CW00348592

Fabulous
MODULAR
ORIGAMI

20 origami models with instructions and diagrams

Tomoko Fuse
the great Japanese origami master

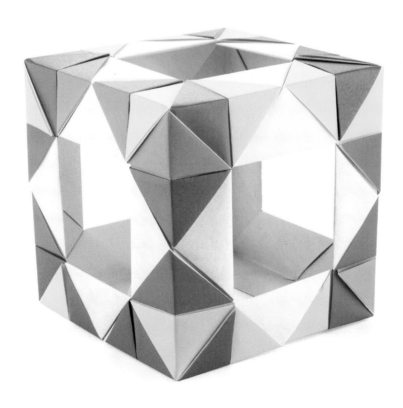

Dover Publications, Inc.
Mineola, New York

Copyright

Copyright © 2017 by NuiNui
NuiNui is a registered trademark of Snake SA, Switzerland
All rights reserved.

Bibliographical Note

Fabulous Modular Origami: 20 Original Models with Instructions and Diagrams,
first published by Dover Publications, Inc., in 2018, is an unabridged English
translation of the work originally published by NuiNui, Switzerland, in 2017.

International Standard Book Number

ISBN-13: 978-0-486-82693-6
ISBN-10: 0-486-82693-7

Manufactured in the United States by LSC Communications
82693701   2018
www.doverpublications.com

Texts and diagrams
Tomoko Fuse

● ●

Photographs
Dario Canova

INTRODUCTION

Among the many joys of making origami, there is one
in particular that makes modular origami stand out:
its distinctive geometric component. However, this does not
necessarily mean that it has to be difficult. There are plenty
of simple and stimulating models that are easy to understand
and can be made by anyone.

Modular origami involves joining different modules made with sheets
folded separately. What is unusual about it is precisely the fact that it
requires two different types of processes, namely folding and assembly.

One intriguing aspect of this type of origami comes from the fact that
glue is not normally used to join the modules together. However, if you
need to strengthen a model, do not hesitate to glue it.

This book contains a wide range of models, from the easiest, made
using only two modules, to those for more expert origami artists that
can require up to thirty modules.

I hope this book will help you discover the two different layers of
enjoyment modular origami can bring: the inherent pleasure in the
creative process involved in making every piece of origami, and the fun
of a jigsaw puzzle.

SUMMARY

· ·

BIOGRAPHY .... page 10

SYMBOLS KEY .... page 12

Square coaster .... page 18

Menko card or pillow .... page 22

Shuriken or ninja star .... page 26

Crown .... page 30

Flower with stand .... page 36

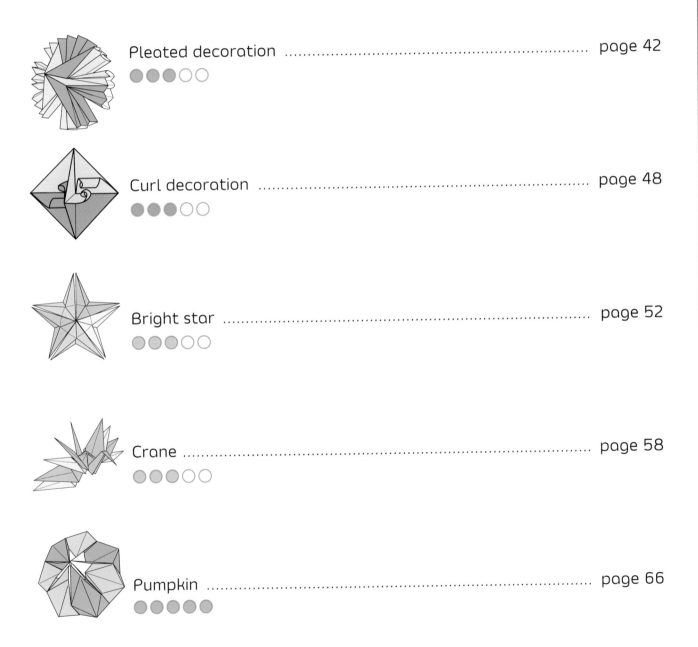

Pleated decoration .... page 42

Curl decoration .... page 48

Bright star .... page 52

Crane .... page 58

Pumpkin .... page 66

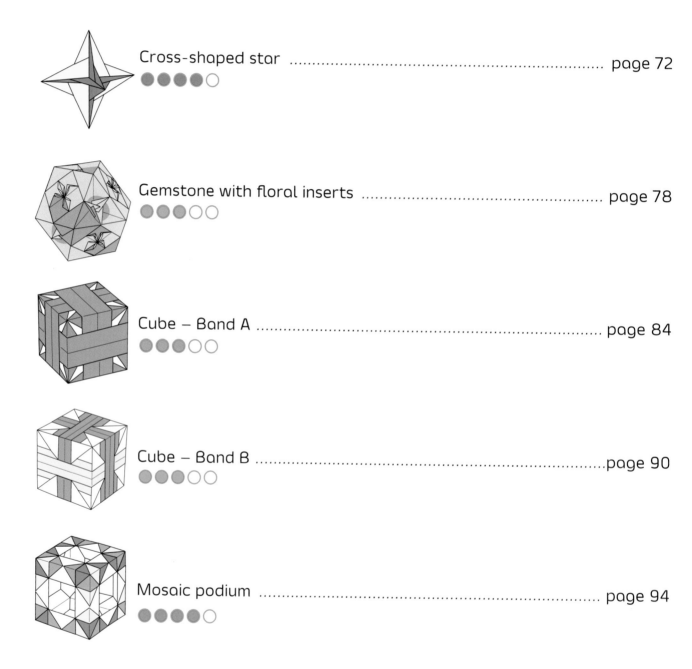

Cross-shaped star .... page 72
●●●●○

Gemstone with floral inserts .... page 78
●●●○○

Cube – Band A .... page 84
●●●○○

Cube – Band B ....page 90
●●●○○

Mosaic podium .... page 94
●●●●○

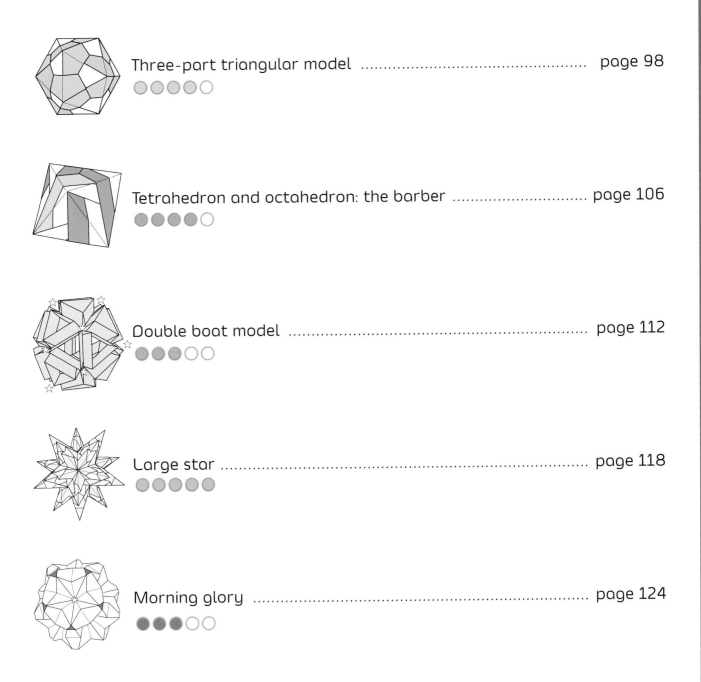

Three-part triangular model .... page 98
⬤⬤⬤⬤◯

Tetrahedron and octahedron: the barber .... page 106
⬤⬤⬤⬤◯

Double boat model .... page 112
⬤⬤⬤◯◯

Large star .... page 118
⬤⬤⬤⬤⬤

Morning glory .... page 124
⬤⬤⬤◯◯

BIOGRAPHY

Tomoko Fuse first came across origami when she was seven years old; she began making paper models during a stay in the hospital. In 1980, well ahead of her time, she became so passionately dedicated to making origami models, using several sheets folded separately, that she earned the nickname "the queen of modular origami."

Constantly experimenting with new ways of folding paper, she began to focus on making geometric shapes and even designed industrial products such as lampshades and the collection of Origami Pots.

1951 She is born in the province of Niigata. She graduates in Garden Design from the University of Chiba.

1986 She moves to Yamamura Yasaka, in the province of Nagano, and begins practising origami professionally.

1987 She is invited to Italy by CDO (Centro Diffusione Origami).

1989 On behalf of the Japan Foundation, she visits the UK, Germany, Holland, Poland and Bulgaria.

1990 She is invited by Origami USA (the American National Association for origami).

1991 She is invited by various organisations and associations to Paris, Germany and Spain.

1994 She organizes the second OSME (an international scientific origami convention) that takes place in Otsu, making a valuable contribution to the success of the event.

1998, 2000, 2003 She is invited to the Festival of Origami in Charlotte, USA.

1998 She is one of three Japanese origami artists invited to exhibit at the Paris origami exhibition held at the Louvre.

1999 She is invited by the Canada Origami Group and the Japanese-German Association.

2002 She is invited to exhibit at the *On Paper* exhibition, held in the UK with sponsorship by the Crafts Council. At the third OSME, which takes place in America, she presents Origami Pots, the result of research conducted with three other colleagues. In the same year, Origami Pots receives a patent.

2003 She is invited to exhibit at the *Origami* exhibition, held at the American Folk Art Museum.

2004 In April, she holds a solo exhibition in Israel, at the Hankin Gallery. In September, she holds another solo exhibition in Germany, at the Bauhaus, and is invited by the British Origami Society.

2005 One of her works is chosen for the poster of the *Masters of Origami* exhibition in Salzburg.

2006 She is invited by the Indian Origami Association.

2008 She is a guest at the general conference held on the occasion of the 25th anniversary of the Dutch Origami Association.

2009 She holds the *Yorokobi* (Happiness) exhibition in Germany, alongside her husband, an artist working with wood.

2010 In March, she is invited by the origami associations of Colombia and Brazil. In August, she is invited by the Ohio CenterFold. In September, she exhibits her origami at the Tokyo Yurakucho Forum. In October, in Germany, to celebrate the centenary of the Fröbel Museum, she once again holds the *Yorokobi* exhibition alongside her husband.

2011 The *Yorokobi* exhibition is transferred to Hittisau, in Austria.

2012 She is one of the artists invited to the travelling American *Folding Paper* exhibition.

2013 In May, she is invited by a group of origami artists in Germany and France. In November she is invited by Mexico Origami.

2014 In July, she is invited by the Ohio CenterFold. In September, on behalf of the Japan Foundation, she visits India and Bhutan. In November, she makes large inlaid models for the Axia South Cikarang Hotel, in Indonesia.

2015 Alongside Heinz Strobl she participates in the *Space Folding* exhibition in Schahof, Germany. In December, she is invited to Italy by the CDO (Centro Diffusione Origami).

2016 In April, she holds a solo exhibition at the Museum of Modern Art Toyoshina in Azumino.

Bibliography

Tomoko Fuse has a hundred books to her name, including *Unit Polyhedron Origami*, *Origami Four Seasons*, *Modular Origami* and *Amazing Origami - Introduction*. Some of these have also been translated into English, German, Italian and Korean. She has also published several essays on life in the mountain village of Yamamura: *Hard-working Mountain Life* and the illustrated volume *Look, what I've Found! Delicacies from the Plains and Mountains*. *Spiral*, a collection of helix, shell and vortex models, was published in 2012.

ftomoko@yasakanet.ne.jp

SYMBOLS KEY

●○○○○	very easy
●●○○○	easy
●●●○○	medium
●●●●○	difficult
●●●●●	expert origami artist

Degree of difficulty

Valley fold

Mountain fold

Fold back

Fold and unfold

Fold into equal parts

Fold so that the
O symbols meet

Fold so that the
• symbols meet

Make a crimp
or accordion fold

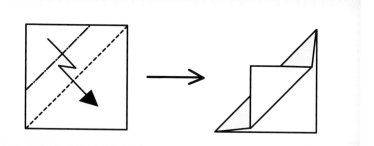

Insert

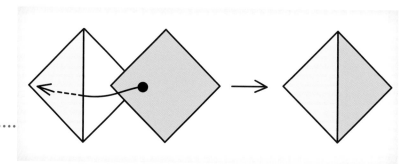

Turn over
the paper

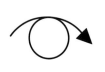

Enlargement

Reduction
in scale

Rotate
the paper

Result after
several modules
have been joined
together

The fold only involves
the upper layer, allow
the lower layer to
come out

Reverse fold

Inside reverse fold

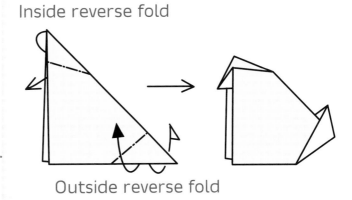

Outside reverse fold

Reverse fold

Inside reverse fold

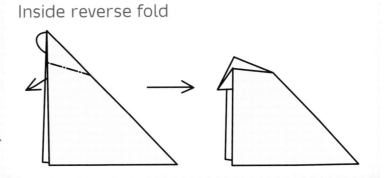

Paper:
standard
15 x 15 cm
(6 inches x 6 inches)

Square coaster

Coaster made by assembling two modules.

As is often the case with modular origami, variations are possible.

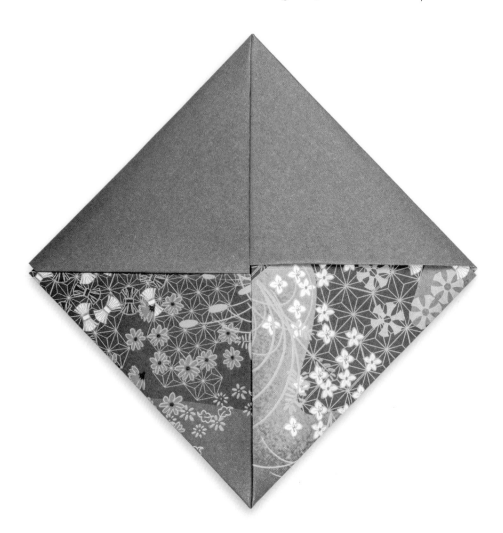

A

①

②

③

Make two.

④

⑤

Joining the modules together.

①

②

Intermediate steps.

③

Insert into the corresponding pockets. Insert the part marked with the ● symbol from above.
Repeat this process on the opposite side with the part marked with the O symbol.

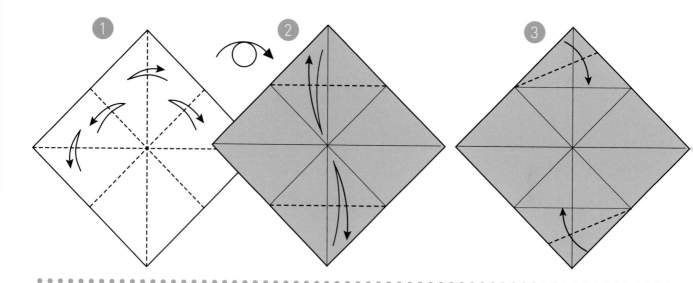

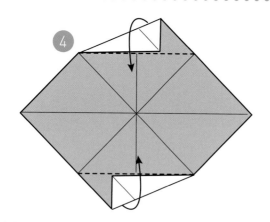 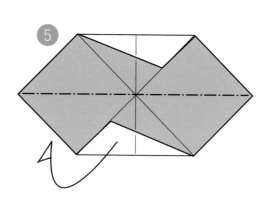

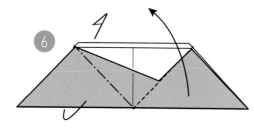 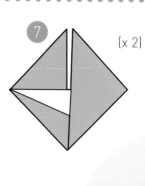

Joining the modules together.

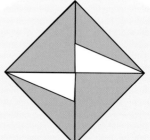

(x 2)

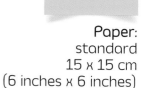

Paper:
standard
15 x 15 cm
(6 inches x 6 inches)

Menko card or pillow

(traditional Japanese origami)

Menko is a traditional game that involves throwing a square or round card of heavy paper onto the ground to flip over your opponent's card.

These cards are made by assembling two sheets of paper folded as a mirror image, or rather one in one way and the other symmetrically.

The *menko* card or pillow requires a certain thickness, but if you decide to use it as a coaster, you could use the rectangle obtained by cutting a square sheet of paper in half.

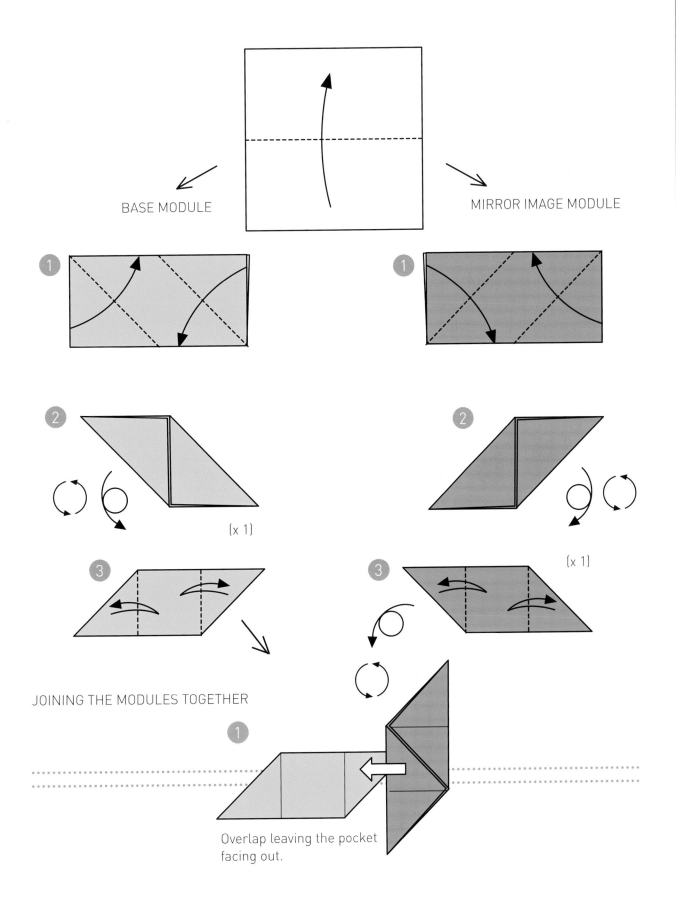

BASE MODULE

MIRROR IMAGE MODULE

(x 1)

(x 1)

JOINING THE MODULES TOGETHER

Overlap leaving the pocket
facing out.

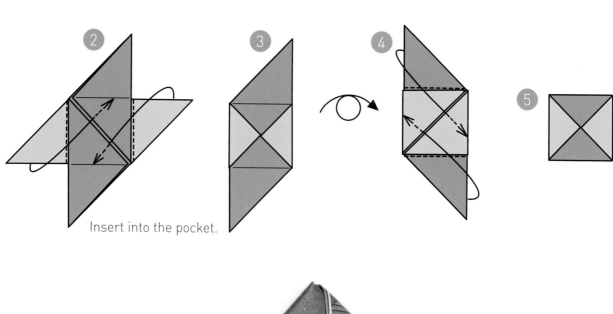

Insert into the pocket.

Paper:
standard
15 x 7.5 cm
(6 inches x 3 inches)

Shuriken or ninja star
(traditional Japanese origami)

Use mirror image modules for this fun piece
of origami with sharp points.

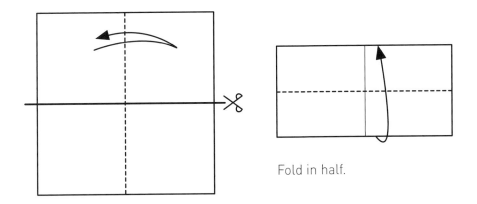

Fold in half.

BASE MODULE

① ② ③ (x 1)

JOINING THE MODULES TOGETHER

Carry out each step with both sheets of paper.

MIRROR IMAGE MODULE

①

②

③

Fold the sheet and pull it down.

Close it around the other sheet, leaving the side with the pocket facing out.

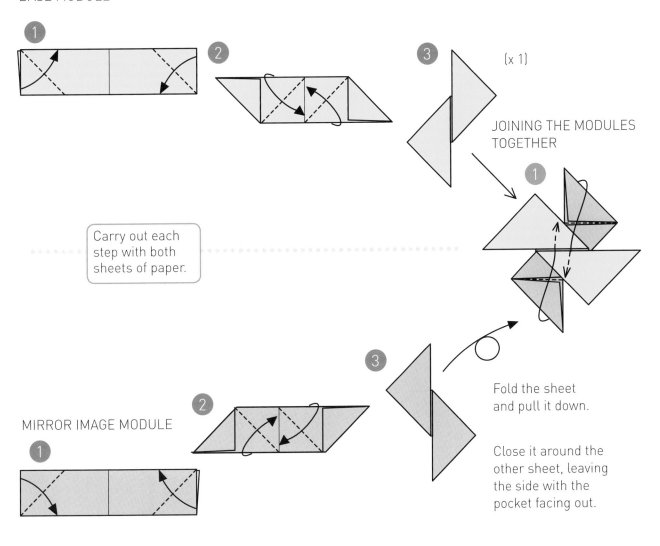

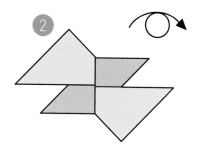 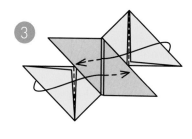 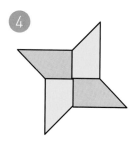

Insert into the respective pockets.

Paper:
standard
15 x 15 cm
(6 inches x 6 inches)

Crown

Easy to make and perfect to wear.

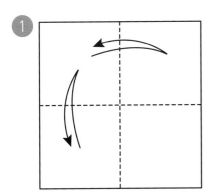

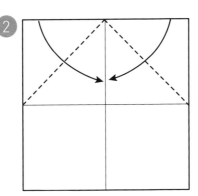

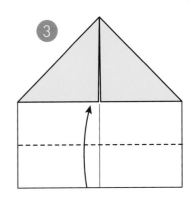

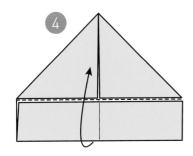

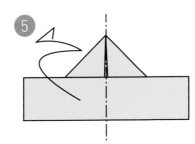

Make a mountain fold.

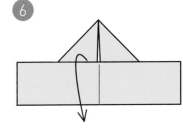

Open temporarily.

(x 7 - x 8)

Increase or reduce the overlap depending on the size of the wearer's head.

JOINING THE MODULES TOGETHER
(diagrams of the outer side)

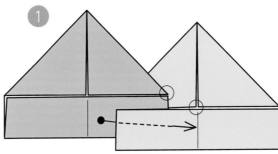

Insert so that the O symbols meet.

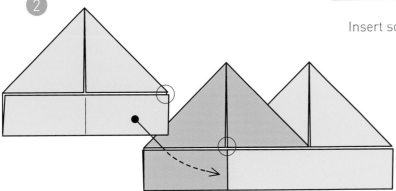

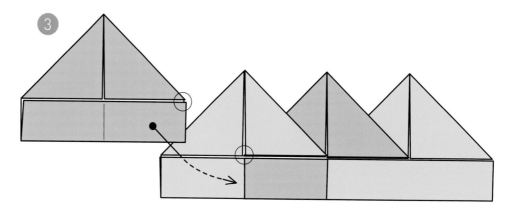

Combine 7-8 modules using
the same process.

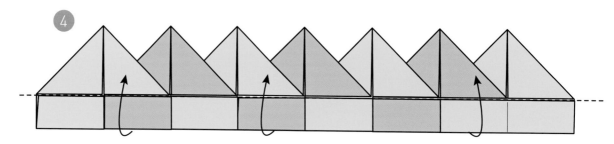

Fold by wrapping the flap around itself.
Make sure the model does not come loose.

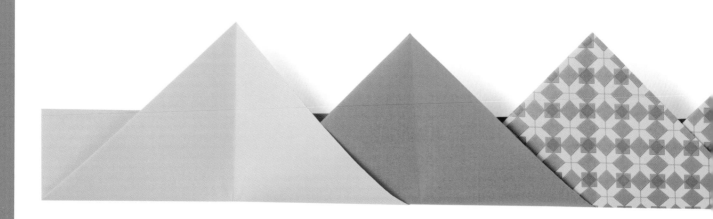

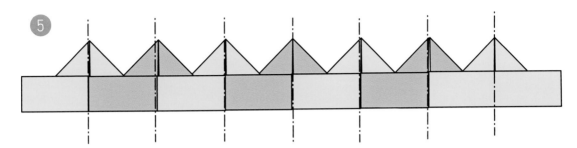

5

Gradually make a mountain fold, creating a circular shape.

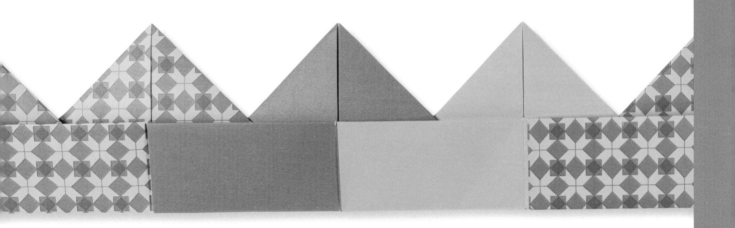

6

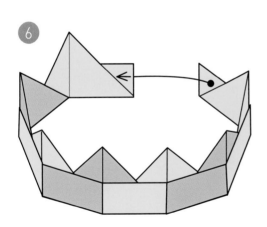

Once you have a circular shape, slot in the ends.

7

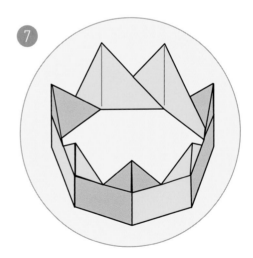

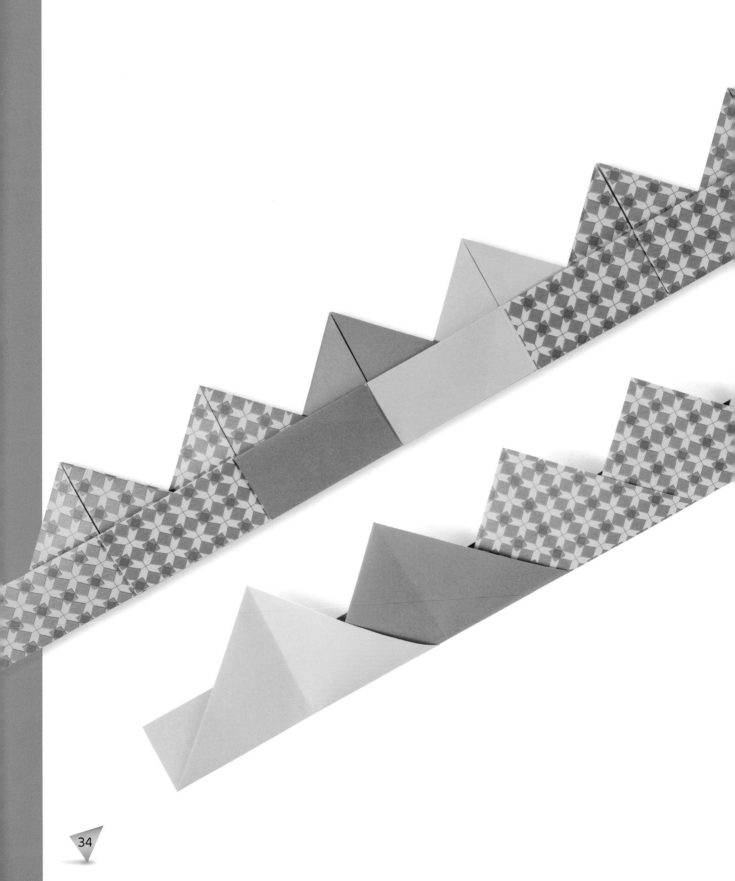

Paper:
standard
15 x 15 cm
(6 inches x 6 inches)

Flower with stand

Rest the flower on a stand that looks like a crown of leaves.
Add a second ring of petals to make the effect even more spectacular.

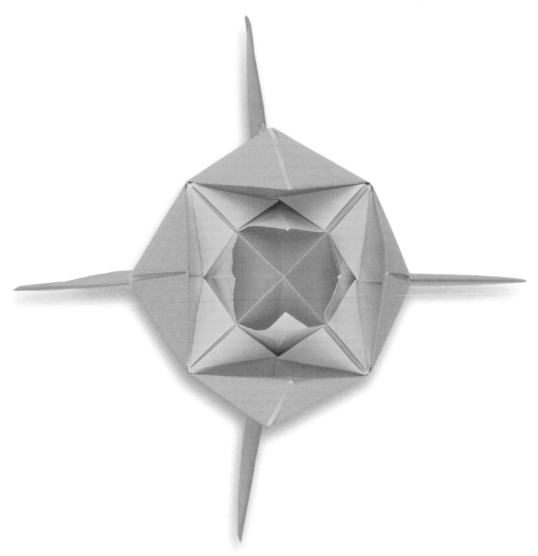

FLOWER A

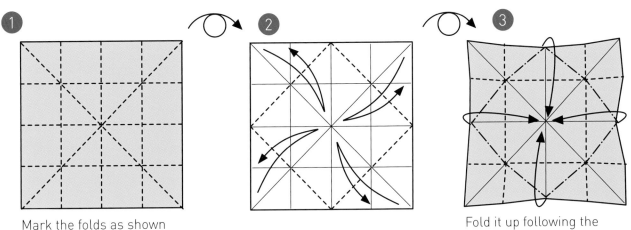

1 Mark the folds as shown in the diagram.

2

3 Fold it up following the lines shown.

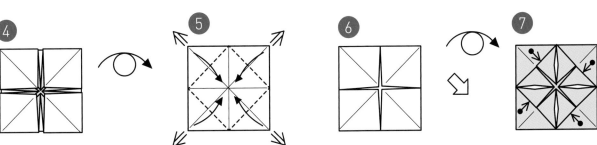

4

5 Lift without folding the layer underneath.

6

7 Poke your finger into all the points marked with the • symbol.

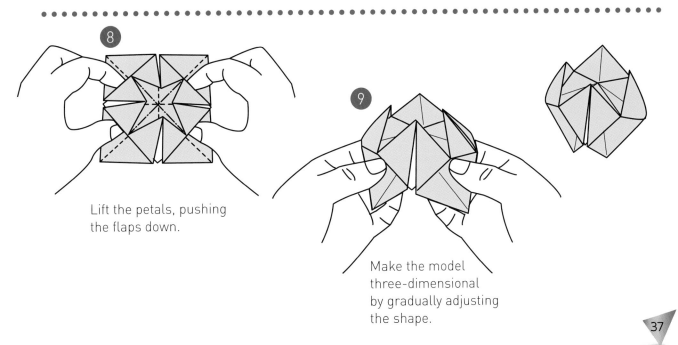

8 Lift the petals, pushing the flaps down.

9 Make the model three-dimensional by gradually adjusting the shape.

LEAVES

STAND

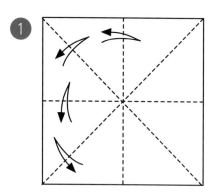

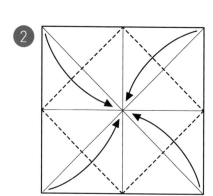

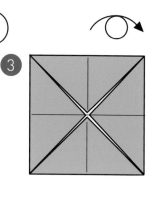

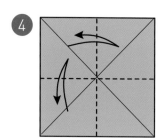

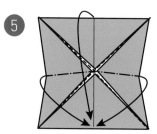

Close up by following
the lines shown to hollow
out the center.

Make a cross shape.

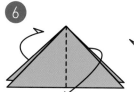

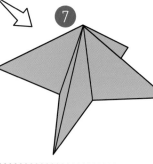

JOINING THE MODULES
TOGETHER
Insert the crown of leaves
into the flower.

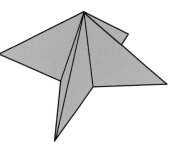

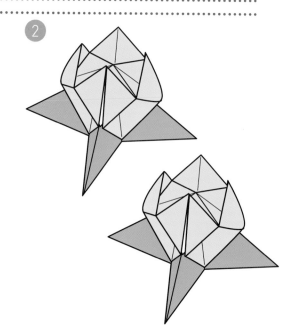

FLOWER B

Add flower B to make the effect even more spectacular.

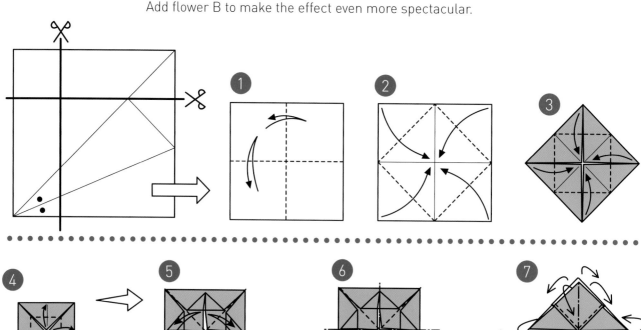

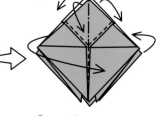

Close up along the
lines shown to make
the center convex.

Open the upper
ring of petals into
a cross shape.

Flatten the
model slightly.

JOINING THE MODULES
TOGETHER

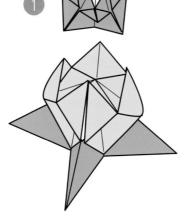

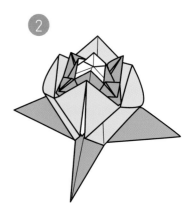

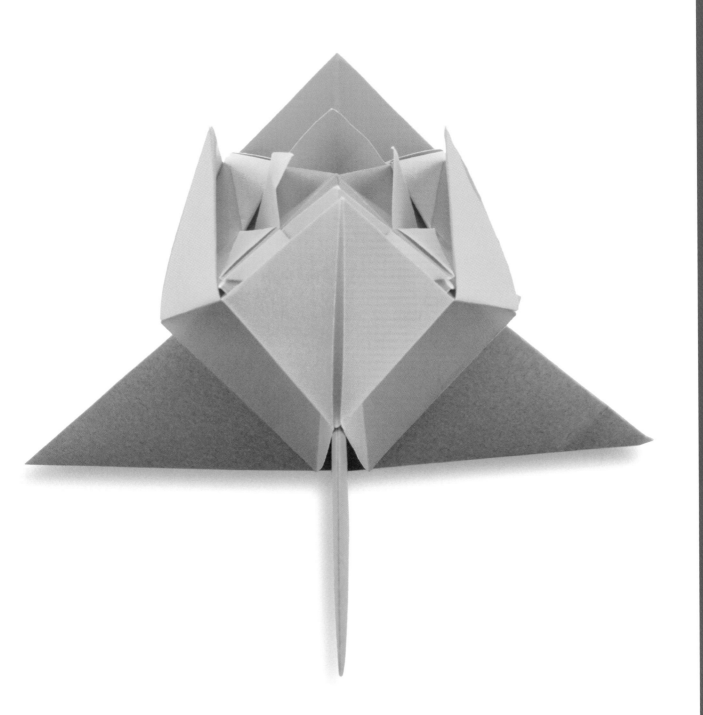

Paper:
standard
15 x 7.5 cm
(6 inches x 3 inches)

Pleated decoration

Create the pleats with a series of crimps.

The folds have a fastener to stop them from working loose.

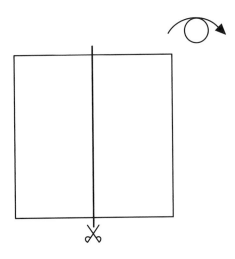

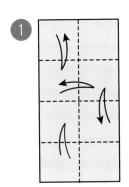

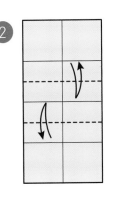

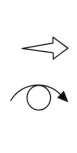

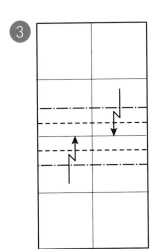

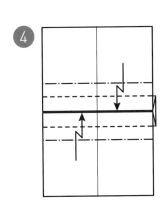

Carry out the crimp creating two symmetrical folds.

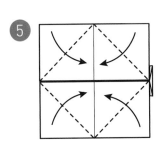

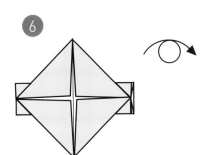

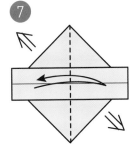

After marking the central fold, open it up in the two places shown.

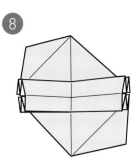

(x 6 or more)

JOINING THE MODULES TOGETHER

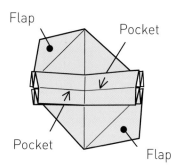

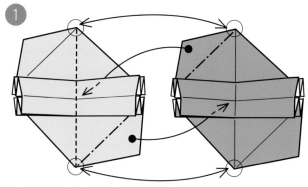

Insert the flaps (symbol •) into the pockets in an alternating fashion so that the O symbols meet. This step will be easier if the left module is folded back.

Once the flaps are inserted, fold and bring together the next module in the same way.

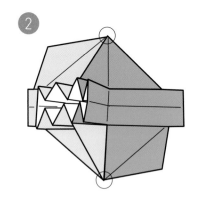

Result when the two modules are joined.

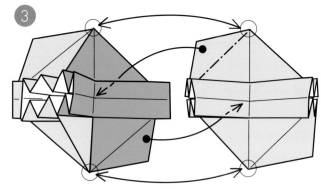

Make a wheel by joining a number of modules.

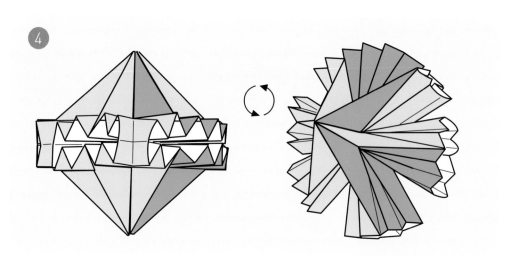

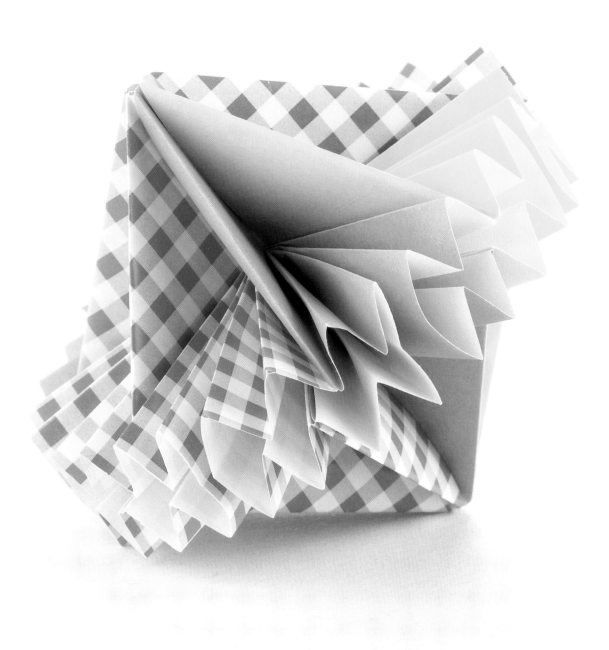

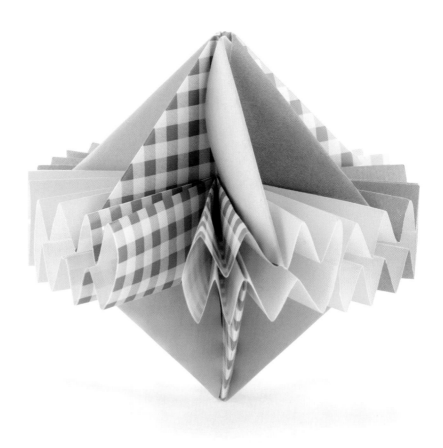

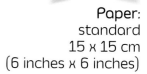

Paper:
standard
15 x 15 cm
(6 inches x 6 inches)

Curl decoration

The paper curls are a key element here.

Make sure they are well-defined. The direction of curl is up to you.

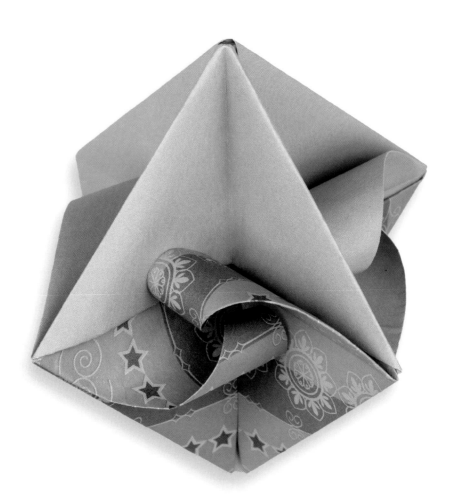

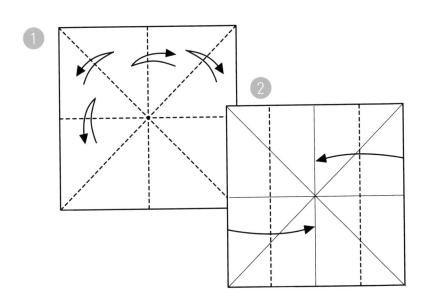

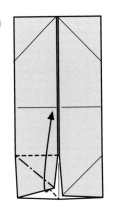

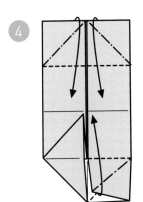

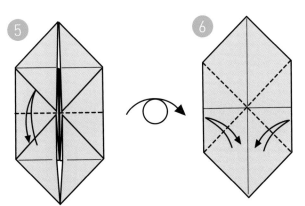

Do the same with the other three corners.

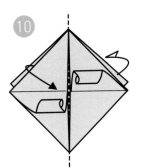

Close it up by following the folds shown.

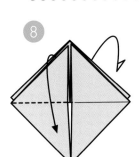

Fold one side down.

Carry out the same process on the opposite side.

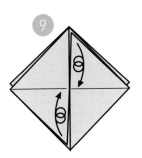

Curl up the tips in whichever direction you prefer.

Open up like a cross.

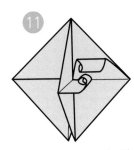

(x 2)

JOINING THE MODULES TOGETHER

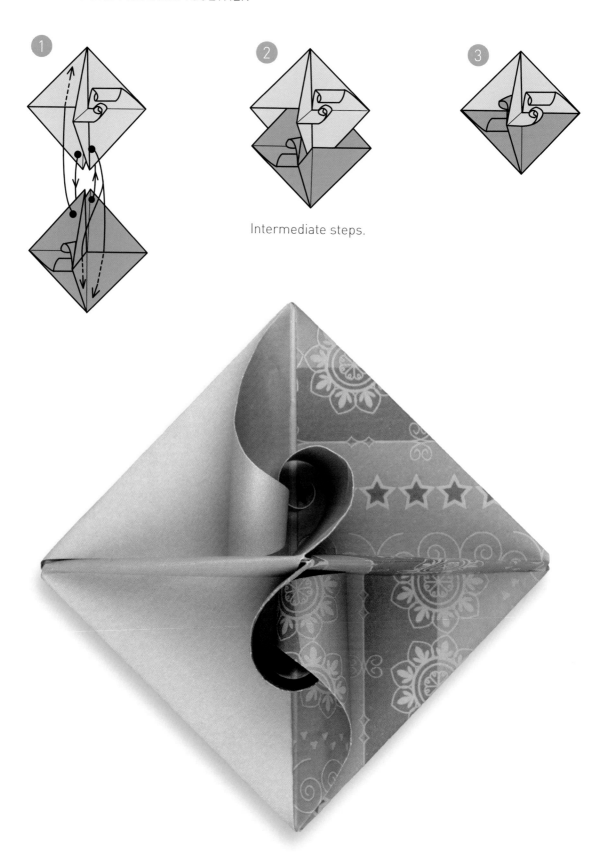

Intermediate steps.

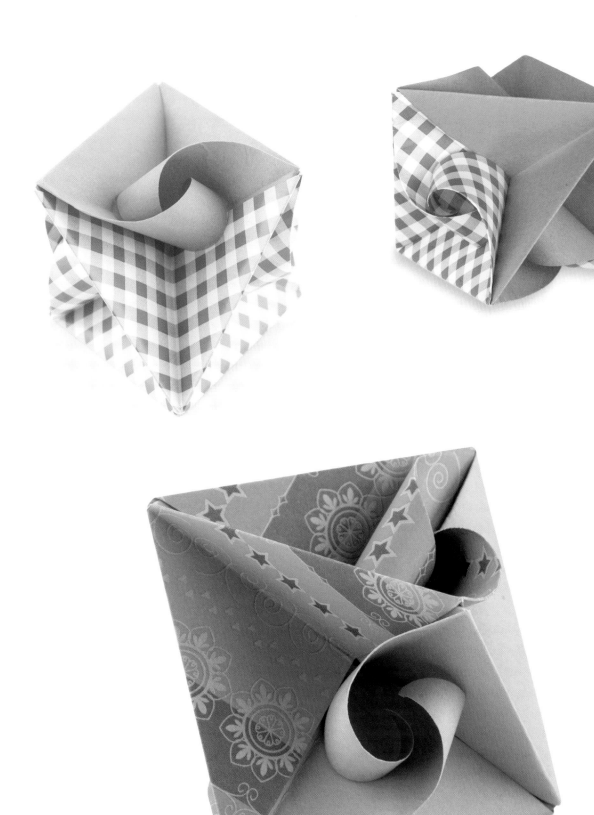

Paper:
standard
7.5 x 7.5 cm
(3 inches x 3 inches)

Bright star

A perfectly dovetailed star.

The double tips are supposed to recreate the twinkling light.

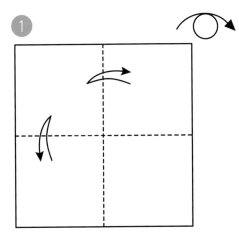

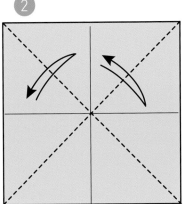

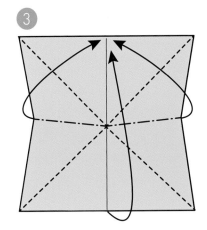

Close it up by following the folds shown.

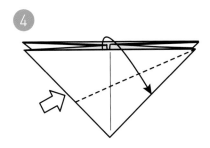

Poke a finger into the point indicated by the arrow, fold the two layers together so the upper right hand edge meets the right side of the triangle.

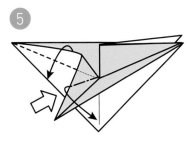

The upper left hand edge must match up with the left side.

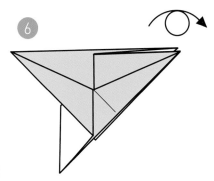

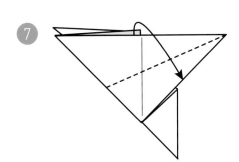

Carry out steps 4 and 5 on the other side.

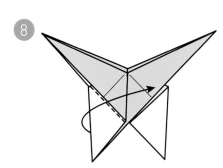

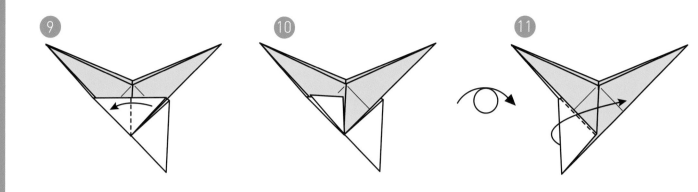

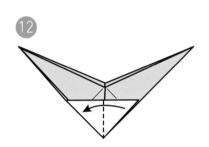

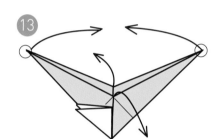

Open in the center and
fold in half, bringing the
O symbols together.

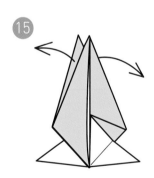

Open carefully.

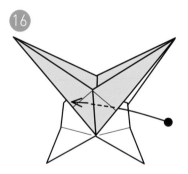

(x 5)

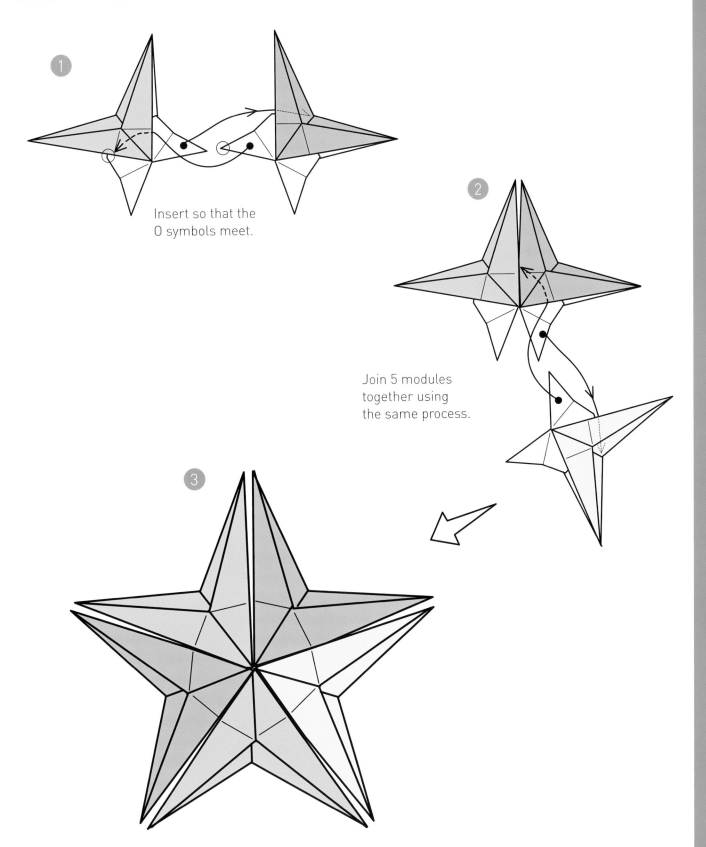

1

Insert so that the
O symbols meet.

2

Join 5 modules
together using
the same process.

3

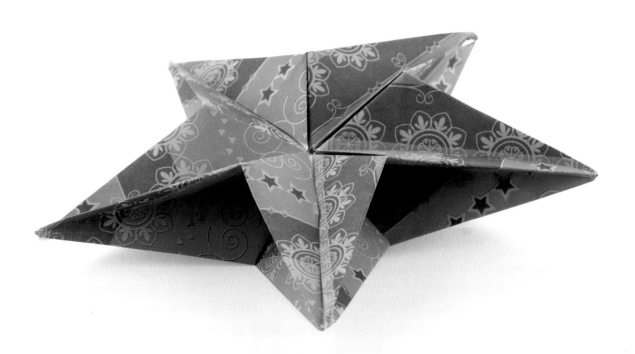

Paper:
standard
15 x 15 cm
(6 inches x 6 inches)

Crane
(traditional Japanese origami)

The crane is the symbol of origami.

Starting with the base model, a variation can be made by inserting extra modules.

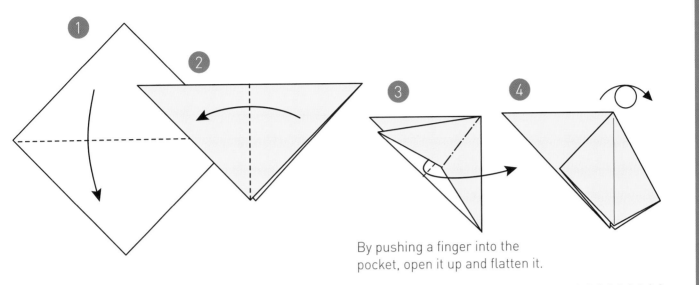

By pushing a finger into the pocket, open it up and flatten it.

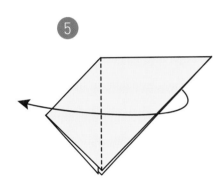

Fold by bringing the triangle to the opposite side.

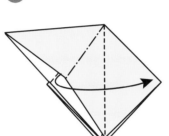

By pushing a finger into the pocket, open it up and flatten it.

Fold and unfold.

Open as much as possible upwards towards the top flap, then flatten the left and right pockets firmly.

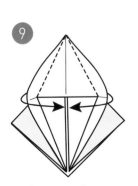

Intermediate steps.

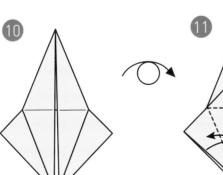

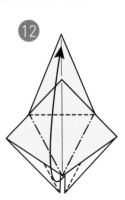

BASE MODEL

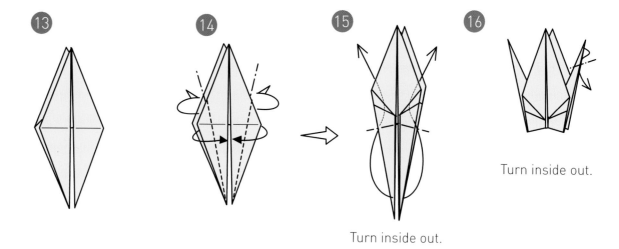

Turn inside out.

Turn inside out.

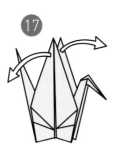

Open the wings
and lift the back.

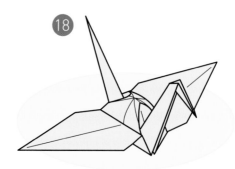

Crane flapping its wings
(variation)

There is a pocket on the back of the crane's wings.
Insert extra wings into it for surprising results.

The sheet must be a quarter of that used for the crane.

EXTRA WING

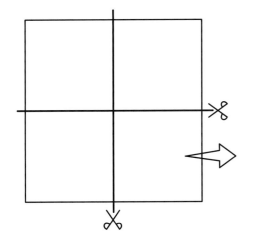 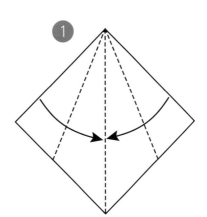 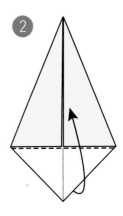

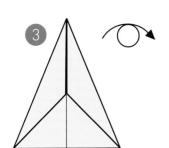 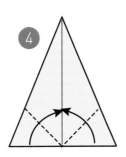 

Open temporarily.

Close it up by following the folds shown.

INTERMEDIATE STEPS

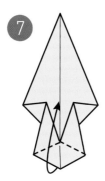

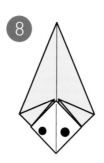

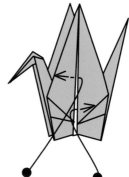

Insert the parts marked with the • symbol.

There is a pocket inside the crane's wings.

....

JOINING THE MODULES TOGETHER

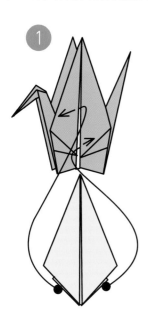

Insert the parts of the extra wing marked with the • symbol into the pocket on the inside of the crane's wing, both left and right.

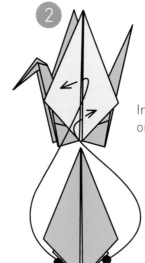

Insert different modules one by one onto the left and right side.

This is the result with three extra wings inserted left and right.

Paper:
standard
15 x 15 cm
(6 inches x 6 inches)

Pumpkin

A curved solid like a pumpkin,
made by joining 5-7 modules.

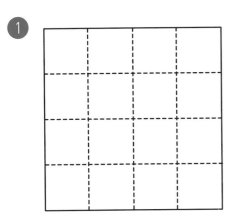

Mark the folds as shown
in the diagram.

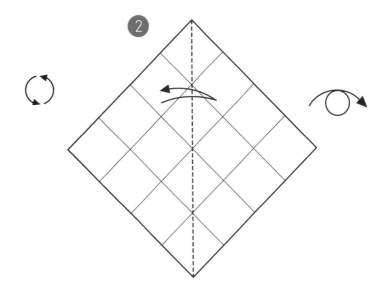

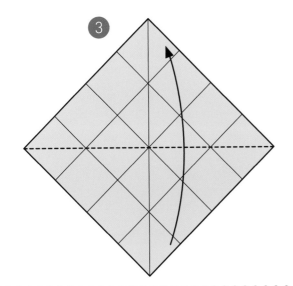

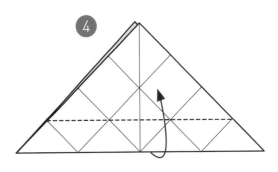

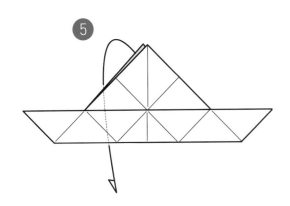

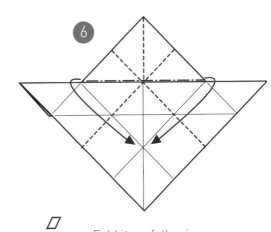

Fold it up following
the lines shown.

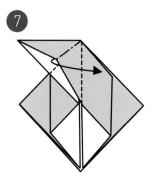

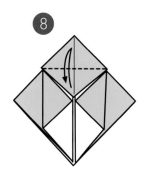

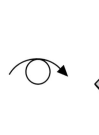

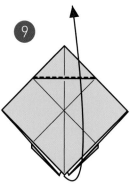

Open the upper layer as much as possible.

INTERMEDIATE STEPS

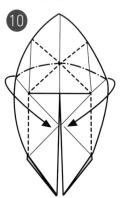

Fold it up following the lines shown.

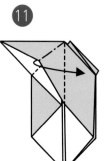

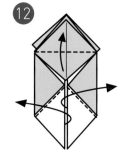

Do not fold the back part of the upper triangle.

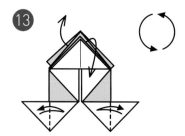

Open up until you see the shape in diagram 14.

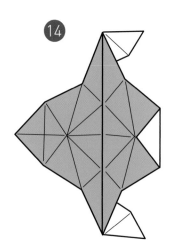

(x 6 - x 7)

JOINING THE MODULES TOGETHER

Module 1 seen from the inside.

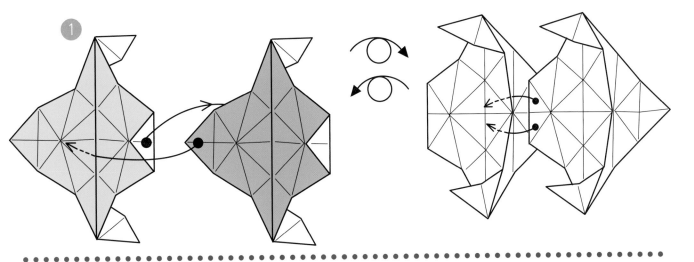

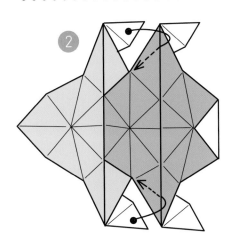

Combine 6-7 modules
using the same process.

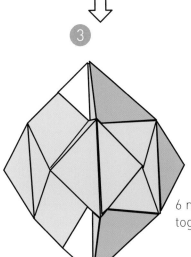

6 modules joined
together.

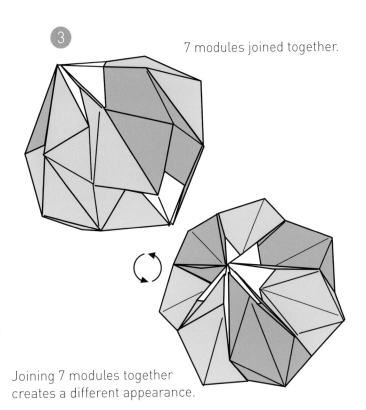

7 modules joined together.

Joining 7 modules together
creates a different appearance.

Paper:
standard
15 x 15 cm
(6 inches x 6 inches)

Cross-shaped star

During the intermediate steps the model appears a little unstable
but once 12 modules are joined together and pushed firmly towards the center,
the sides and corners will automatically fall into place.
Try not to use any glue!

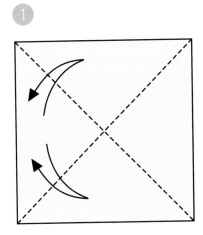

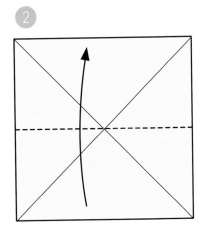

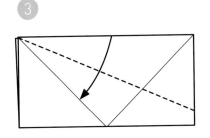

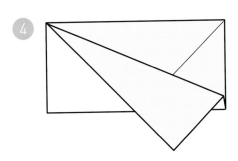

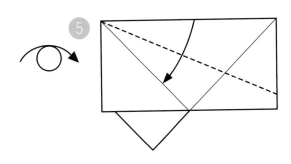

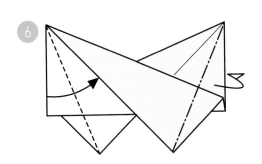

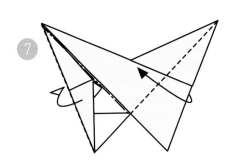

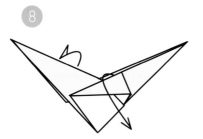

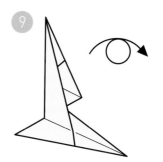

Open the fold
at right angles.

(x 12)

Position of the pocket.

Flap.

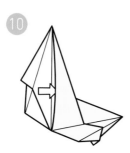

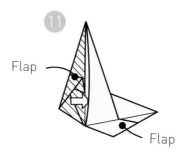

Flap

Flap

Insert into the pocket at
the point shown by the arrow.
Each module joined involves
two insertions.

Insert the two diagonal
flaps into the pocket, as
if they were a single layer.

JOINING THE MODULES TOGETHER

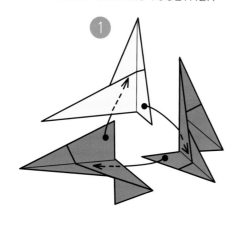

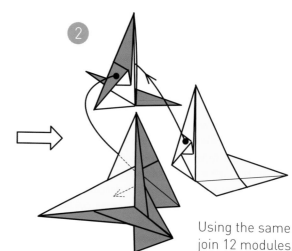

Using the same process
join 12 modules, making
sure the points are arranged
in a cross shape.

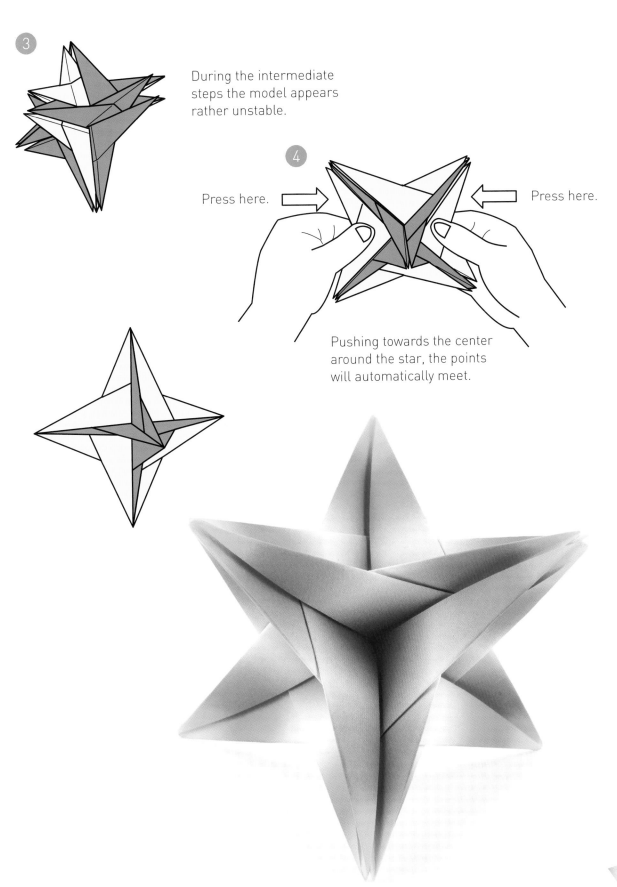

3

During the intermediate steps the model appears rather unstable.

4

Press here. ⇨ ⇦ Press here.

Pushing towards the center around the star, the points will automatically meet.

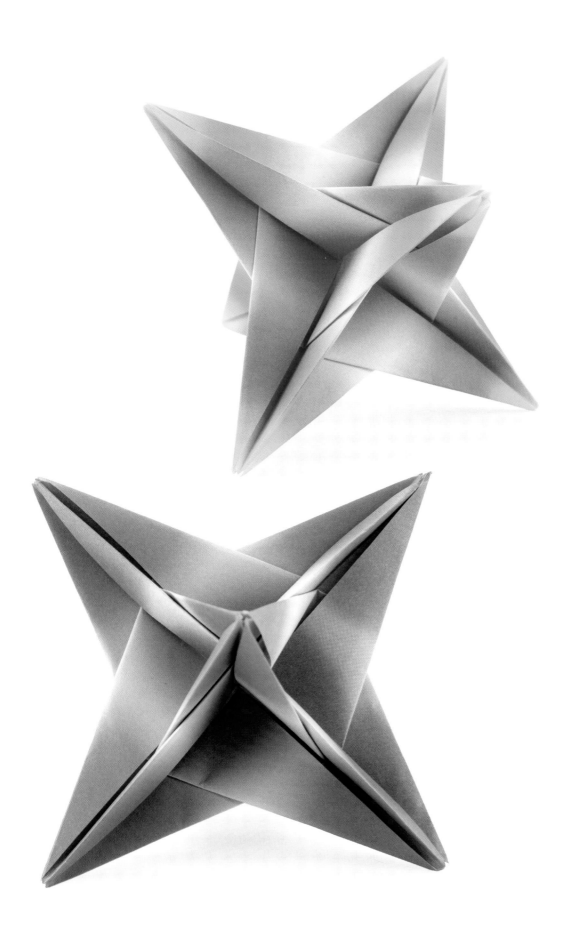

Paper:
standard
15 x 15 cm
(6 inches x 6 inches)

Gemstone with floral inserts

Squares with triangular inserts decorate this modular prism.

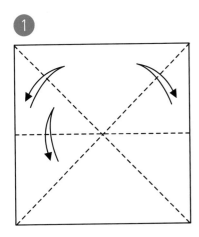

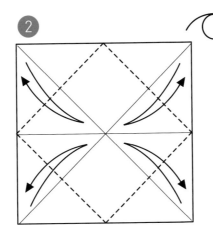

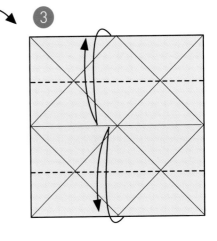

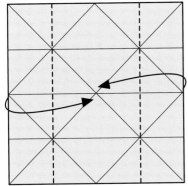

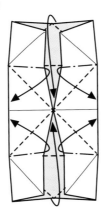

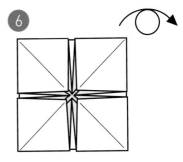

Close it up by
following the
folds shown.

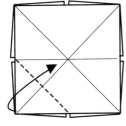

Lift without folding
the layer underneath.

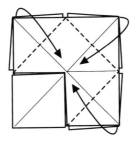

Carry out the same
step at the other
three corners.

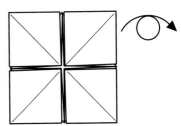

 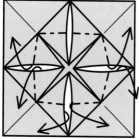 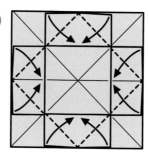 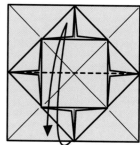

Fold by opening up
the inside.

Mark the folds again
clearly.

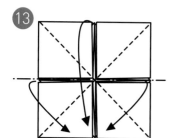

Close it up by following
the folds shown.

After marking the folds
clearly, open up.

(x 12)

JOINING THE MODULES
TOGETHER

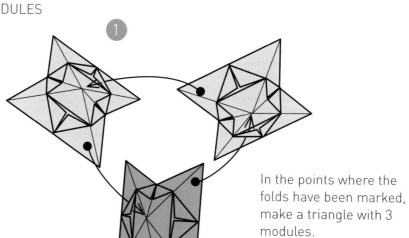

In the points where the
folds have been marked,
make a triangle with 3
modules.

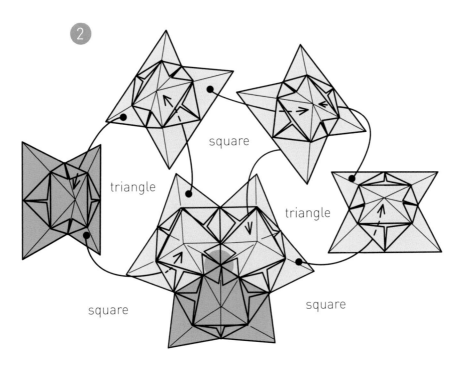

2

square

triangle

triangle

square

square

In the points without folds, join
4 modules to make a square.

3

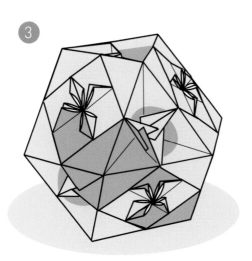

Once the 12 modules have been joined, the
decorative motifs will be in the right position.

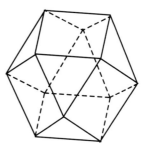

Structure.

Paper:
standard
15 x 15 cm
(6 inches x 6 inches)

Cube – Band A

The bands wrapping the cube can be made in a variety of ways.

This is the fun of origami!

Band A-1

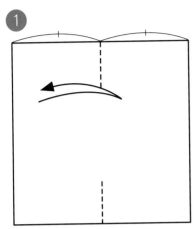

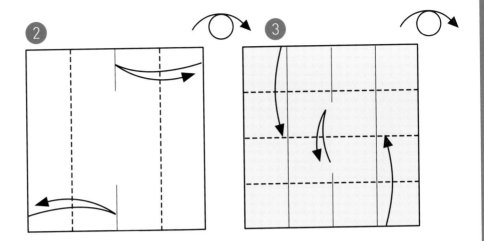

Mark the fold at the ends
only (the final result will
be better).

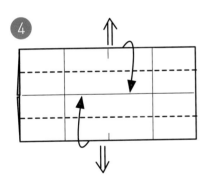

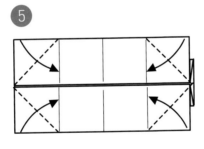

Lift without folding the
layer underneath.

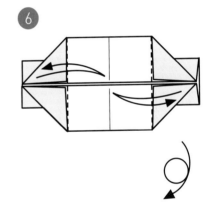

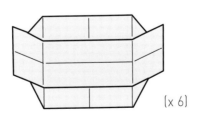

(x 6)

JOINING THE MODULES TOGETHER

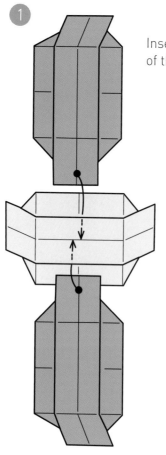

Insert into the pockets of the central band.

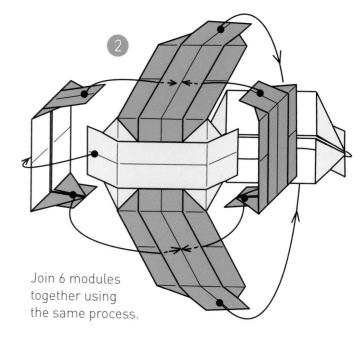

Join 6 modules together using the same process.

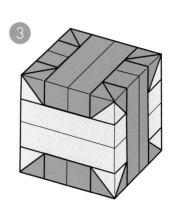

Band A-2

From step 5 of Band A-1

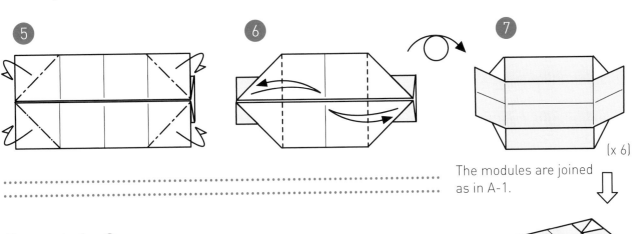

(x 6)

The modules are joined as in A-1.

Band A-3

From step 5 of Band A-1

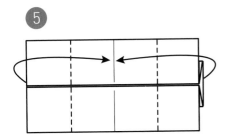
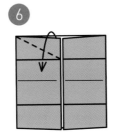
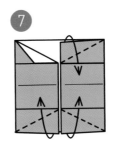
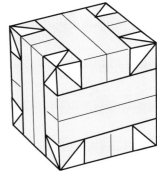

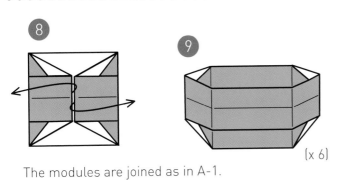

(x 6)

The modules are joined as in A-1.

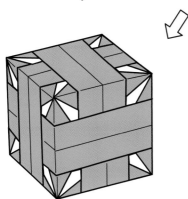

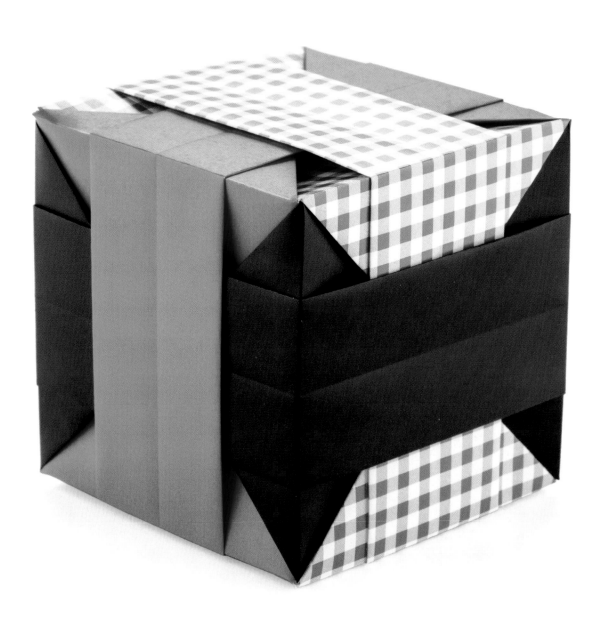

Cube – Band B

Paper:
standard
15 x 15 cm
(6 inches x 6 inches)

This band is smaller than band A and also offers plenty of variation.

Band B-1

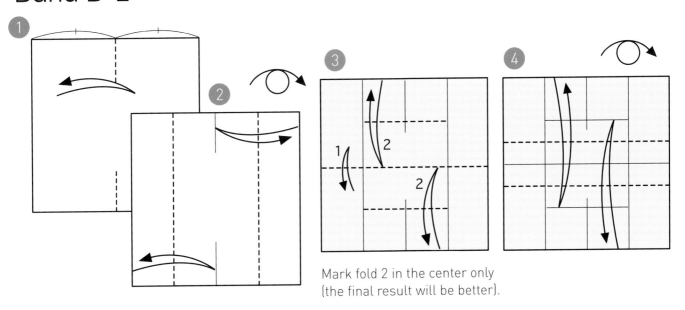

Mark fold 2 in the center only
(the final result will be better).

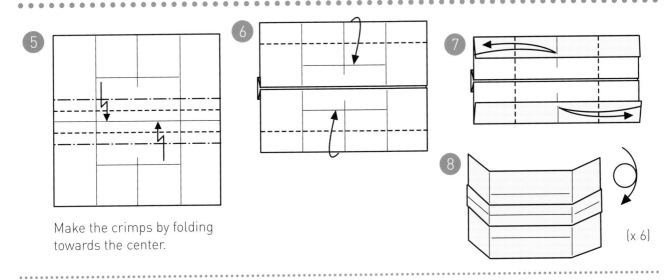

Make the crimps by folding
towards the center.

(x 6)

JOINING THE MODULES TOGETHER

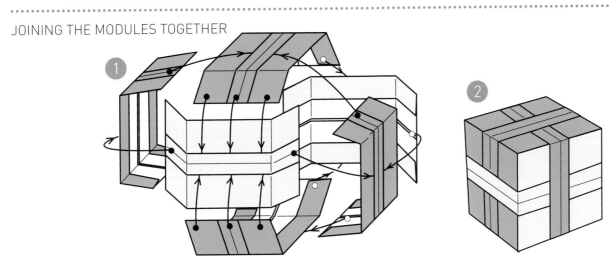

Band B-2

From step 7 of Band B-1

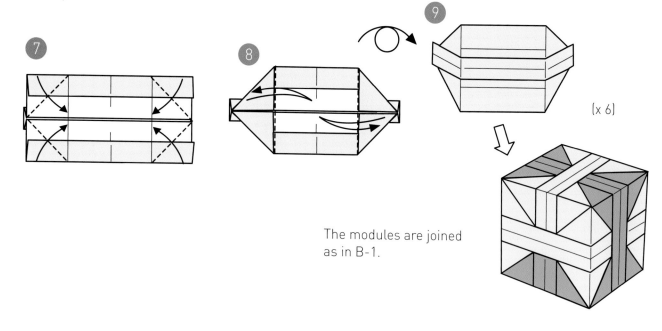

The modules are joined as in B-1.

(x 6)

Band B-3

From step 6 of Band B-1

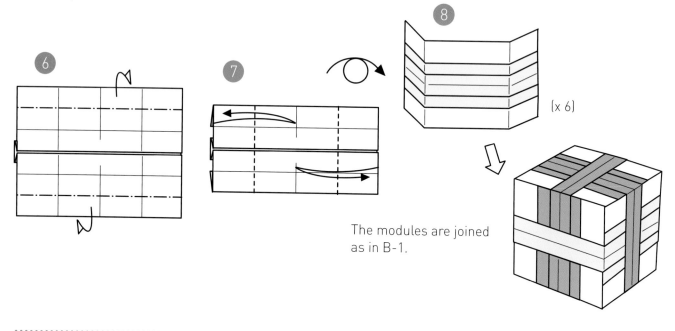

The modules are joined as in B-1.

(x 6)

Band B-4

From step 7 of Band B-3

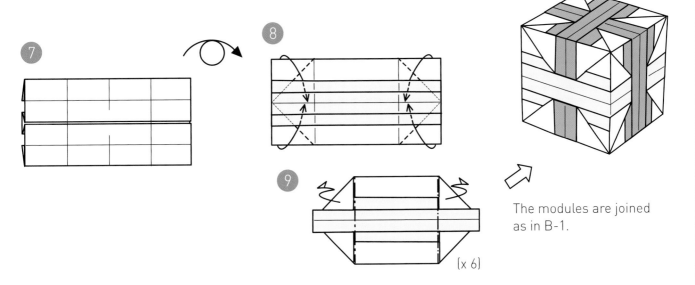

The modules are joined
as in B-1.

(x 6)

Paper:
standard
15 x 15 cm
(6 inches x 6 inches)

Mosaic podium

A model with an origami mosaic pattern.

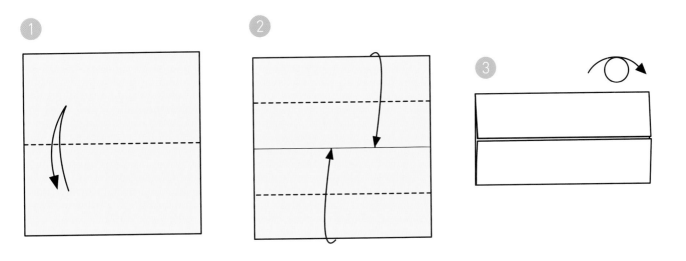

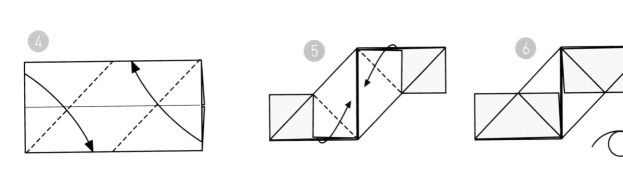

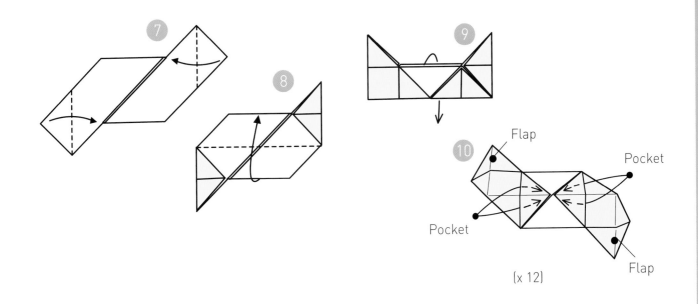

Flap

Pocket

Pocket

Flap

(x 12)

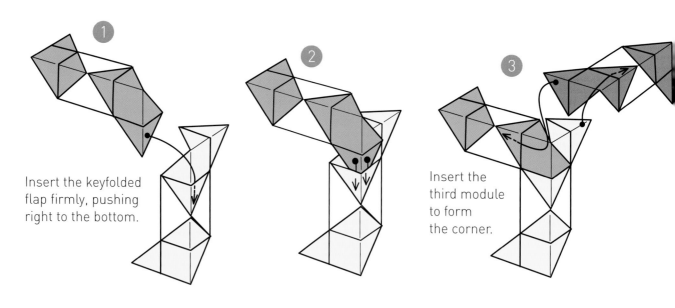

1 Insert the keyfolded flap firmly, pushing right to the bottom.

2

3 Insert the third module to form the corner.

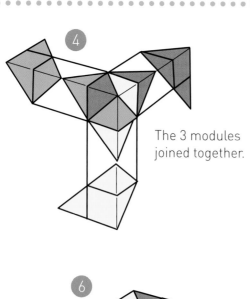

4 The 3 modules joined together.

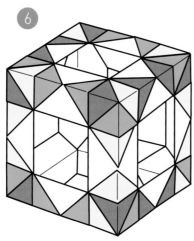

6

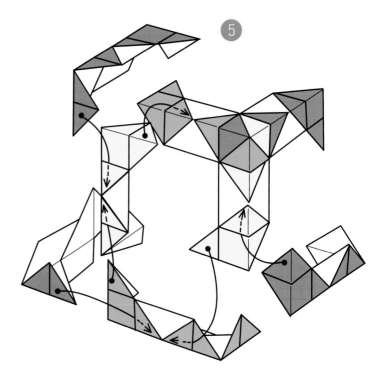

5 Join 12 modules together using the same process.

Paper:
standard
15 x 15 cm
(6 inches x 6 inches)

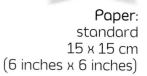

Three-part triangular model

This model consists of three equilateral triangles. For the regular tetrahedron and icosahedron, mirror image modules are used, made by symmetrical left-right folds. Each face will have three parts once the modules are joined together.

Base module

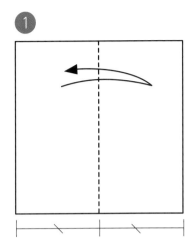

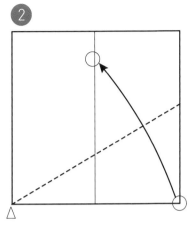

Fold along the axis marked by the △ symbol, bringing the O symbols together.

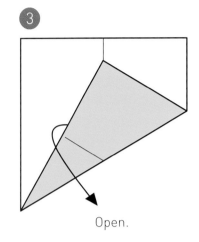

Open.

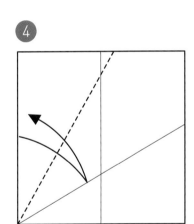

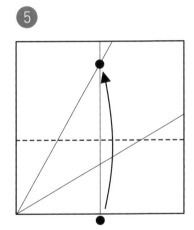

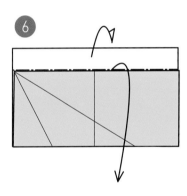

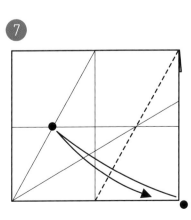

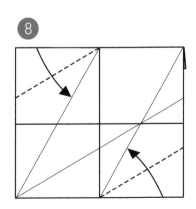

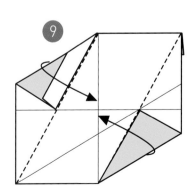

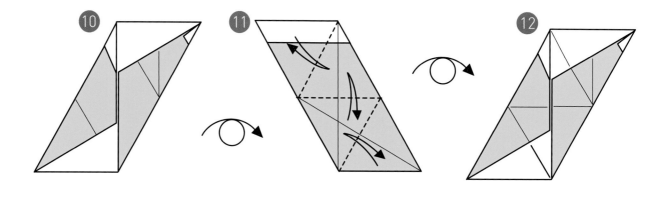

Mirror image module

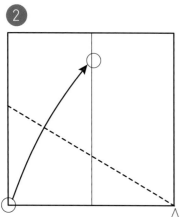

Fold along the axis marked
by the △ symbol, bringing
the O symbols together.

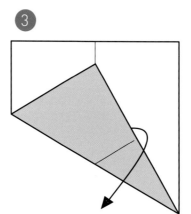

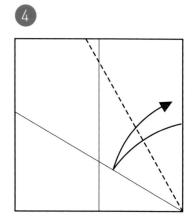

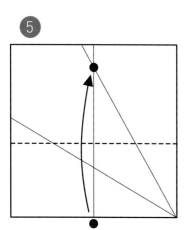

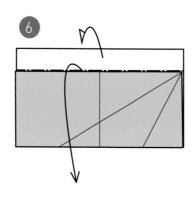

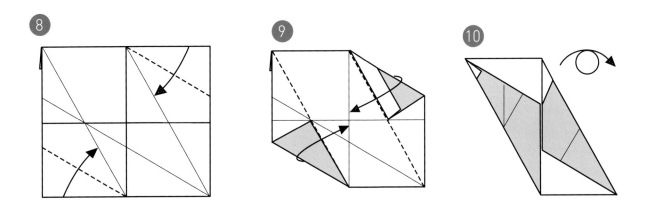

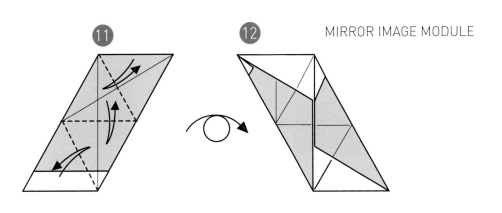

MIRROR IMAGE MODULE

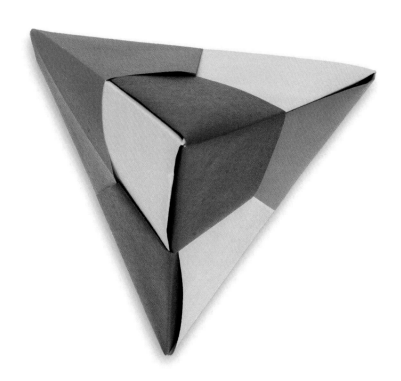

Regular tetrahedron

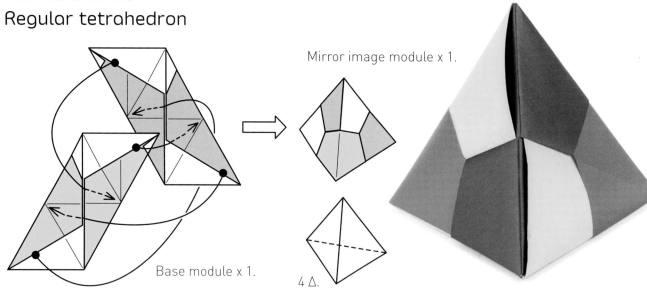

Mirror image module x 1.

Base module x 1.

4 △.

. . . .

Regular octahedron

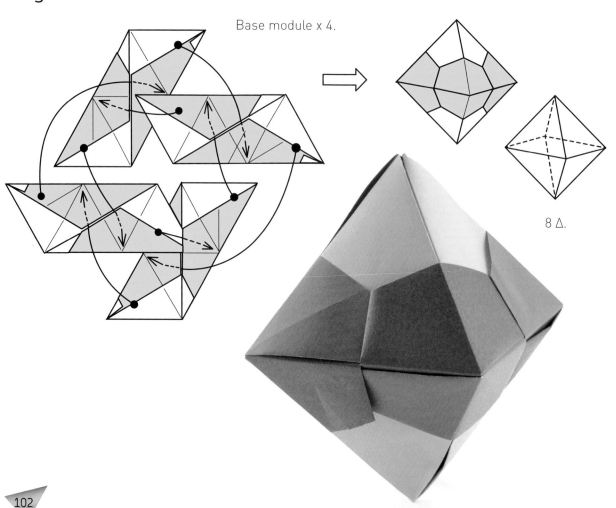

Base module x 4.

8 △.

Regular icosahedron

To make the icosahedron, make two hemispheres, one above and one below, each formed of 5 base modules and 5 mirror image modules, then join these hemispheres together.

Leave this part open then slide it under the adjacent triangle to make the hold firmer.

Base module x 5.

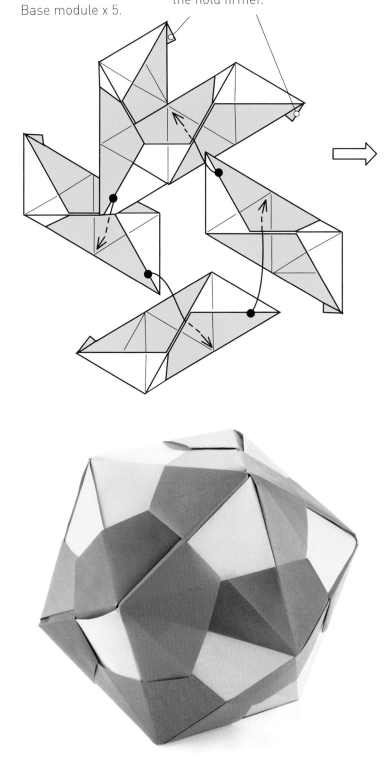

Base module x 5.

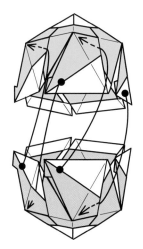

Mirror image module x 5.

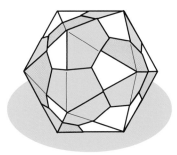

20 Δ.

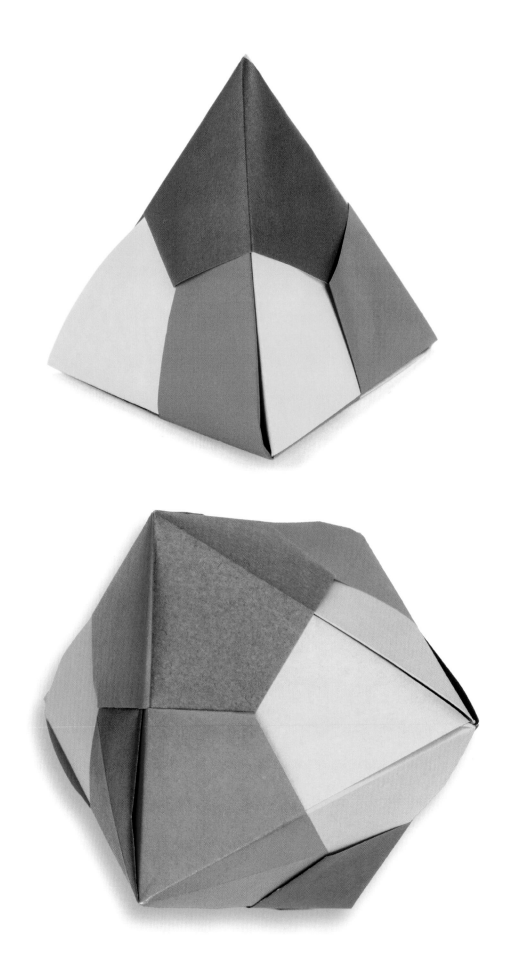

Paper:
standard
15 x 15 cm
(6 inches x 6 inches)

Tetrahedron and octahedron: the barber

A model that is relatively easy to create and join that also involves making mirror image modules, even allowing beginners to experience the fun of modular origami. The name comes from the fact that the stripes of the 6 modules are reminiscent of the red and blue spiral stripes around the column traditionally used as a sign by barber shops.

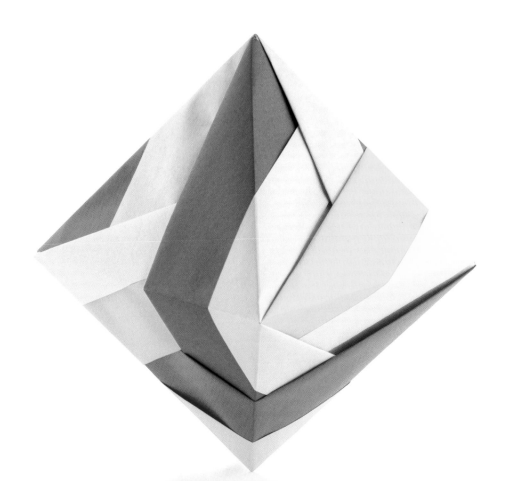

Base module

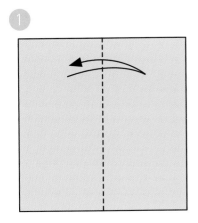

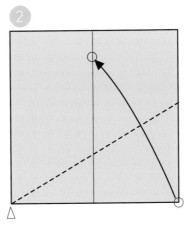

Fold along the axis marked by the △ symbol, bringing the O symbols together.

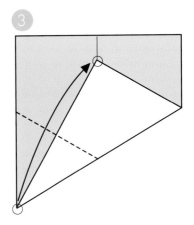

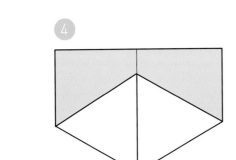

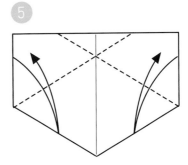

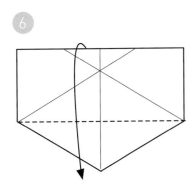

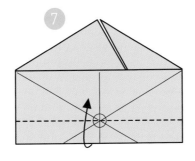

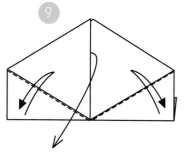

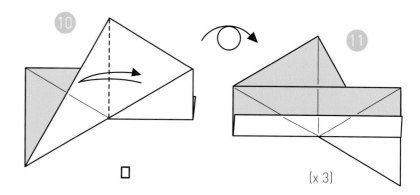

After marking the folds,
open the left hand part.

(x 3)

Mirror image module

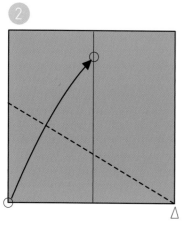

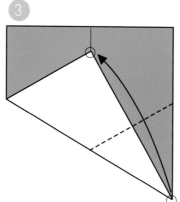

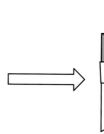

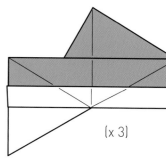

Now fold symmetrically beginning
with step 4 of the "base module."

(x 3)

The regular tetrahedron   3 MODULES JOINED TOGETHER

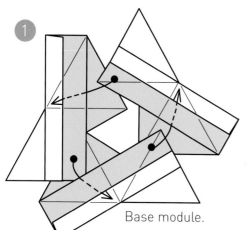

Base module.

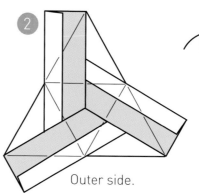

Outer side.

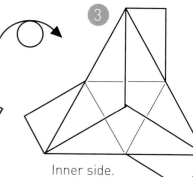

Inner side.

POSITION OF POCKETS AND FLAPS

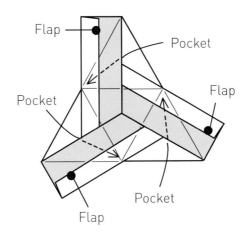

Flap

Pocket

Flap

Pocket

Pocket

Flap

JOINING THE MODULES TOGETHER

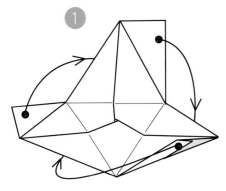

1

Insert by aligning the points of the triangles.

2

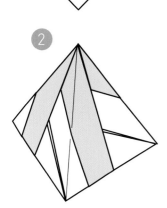

The regular tetrahedron.

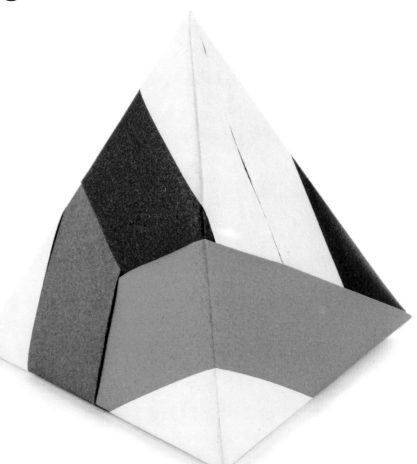

The regular octahedron

1: first join 3 base modules and 3 mirror image modules.
2: aligning the top, bottom, and center of the module and its mirror image will make an octahedron.

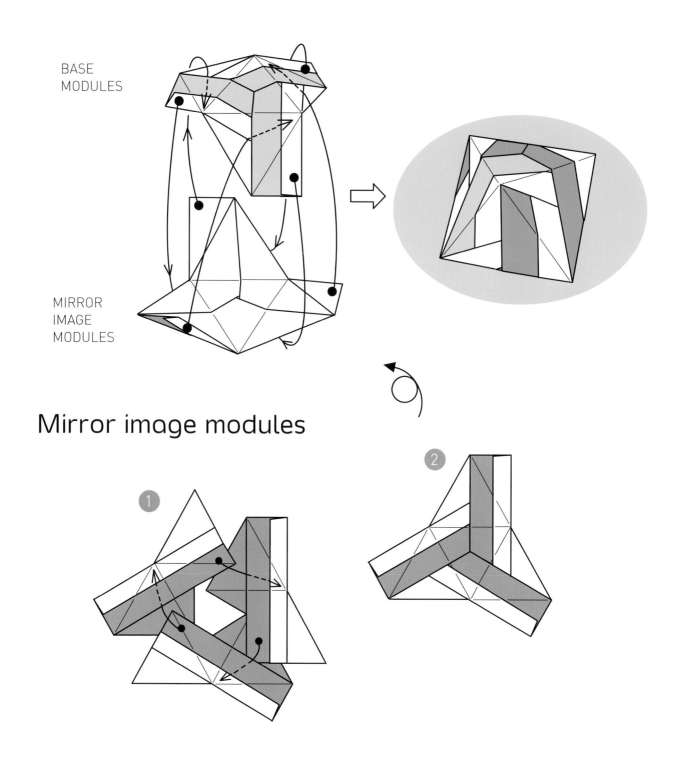

BASE
MODULES

MIRROR
IMAGE
MODULES

Mirror image modules

Paper:
standard
7.5 x 7.5 cm
(3 inches x 3 inches)

Double boat model

A model that incorporates the traditional "double boat."
There are lots of different ways to join the modules in addition
to the one shown here.

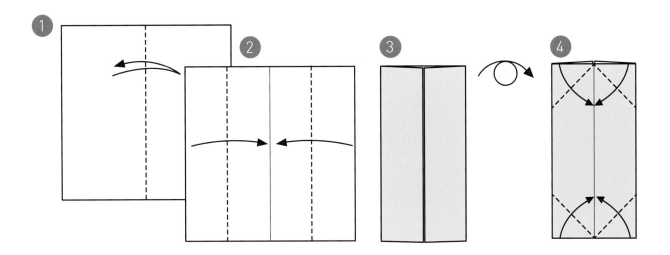

Intermediate step.

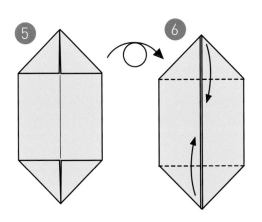

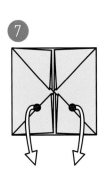

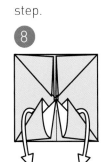

Lift only one layer of the triangles and then lower.

Fold in half at point 10 to create the traditional "double boat."

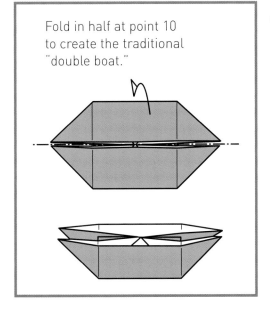

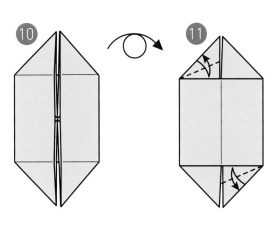

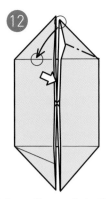
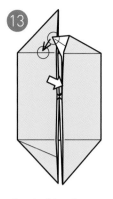

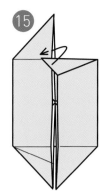

Poke a finger into the point indicated by the arrow and run it down towards the bottom. Fold along the fold created in step 11 so that the O symbols meet.

Insert the point into the top pocket.

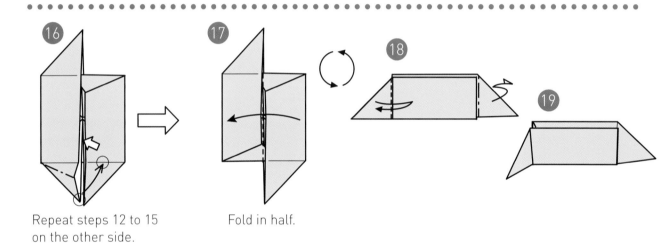

Repeat steps 12 to 15 on the other side.

Fold in half.

JOINING THE MODULES TOGETHER

3 base modules joined together.

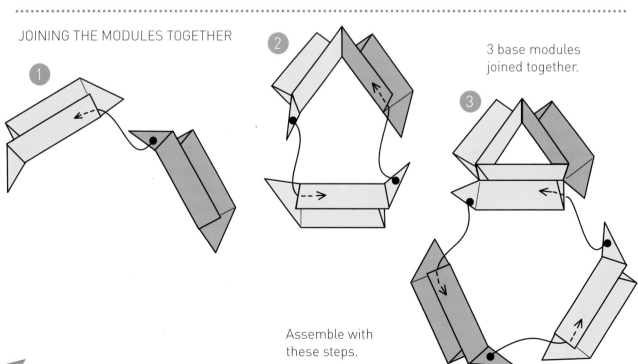

Assemble with these steps.

12 MODULES JOINED TOGETHER

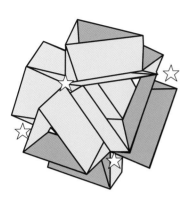

Structure created by joining 12 modules together.

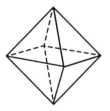

Join together so that 4 modules meet at the points marked by the ☆ symbol.

30 MODULES JOINED TOGETHER

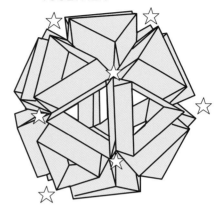

Structure created by joining 30 modules together.

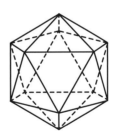

Join together so that 5 modules meet at the points marked by the ☆ symbol.

Paper:
standard
10 x 10 cm
(4 inches x 4 inches)

Large star

When you look at this star, many of you will be reminded of the work of the origami artist Paolo Bascetta. My idea was to create a simple and sturdy star modeled on those created by the Italian master. Here's the result. I've called it "Large star" because, compared to the size of the sheet of paper used, you can create a surprisingly large model. The most suitable size of sheet is given above.

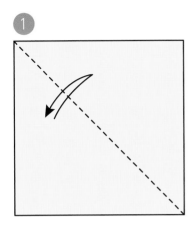

Mark the folds.

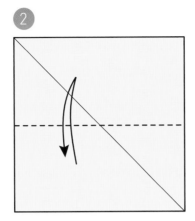

Fold so that the O symbols meet.

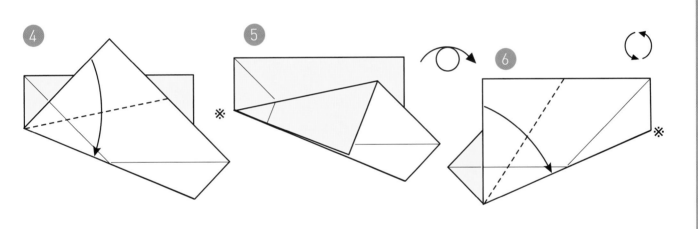

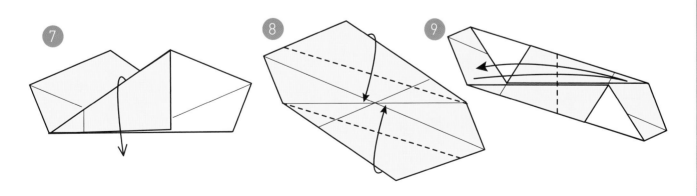

119

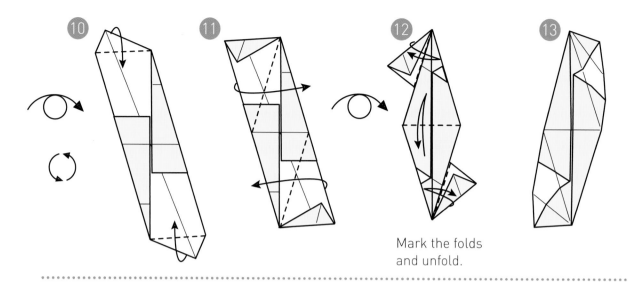

Mark the folds
and unfold.

JOINING THE MODULES TOGETHER

3 base modules joined together.

Insert the points one
below the other, as if
wrapping them.

These are the 3 modules
arranged like a pyramid.
The base of the pyramid
is an equilateral triangle.

30 modules.

The explanation as to how
to join 12 and 30 modules
using the same process
is on the following page.

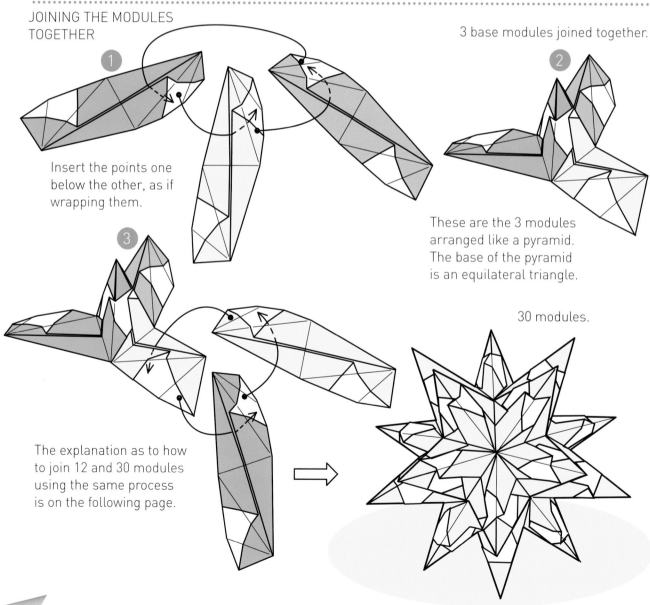

Structure with 12 modules.

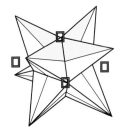

Bring together so the edges of 4 modules meet at each ☆ symbol. Position the colored sections as shown in the diagram.

The base of the pyramid is an equilateral triangle.

Structure with 30 modules.

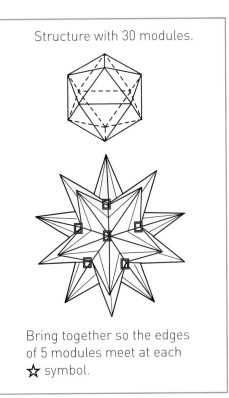

Bring together so the edges of 5 modules meet at each ☆ symbol.

Decorated star

You can make a different variation of this star by turning up the flaps slightly and curling them.

From diagram 8 of the Large star.

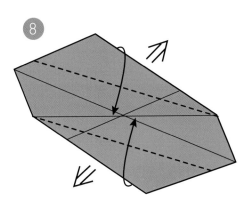

Lift without folding the layer underneath.

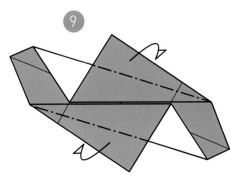

Fold by wrapping between the two flaps.

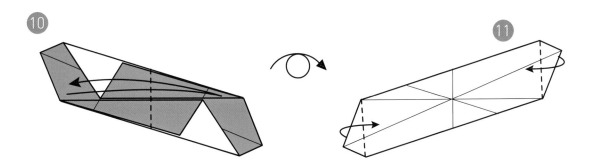

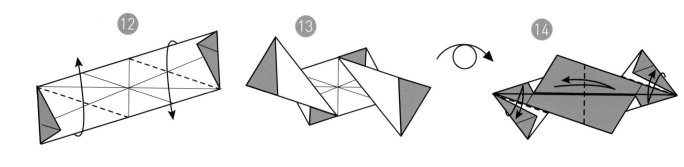

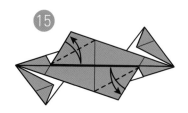
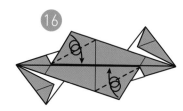
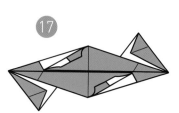

Fold by wrapping between the two flaps.

JOINING THE MODULES TOGETHER

Base modules joined together.

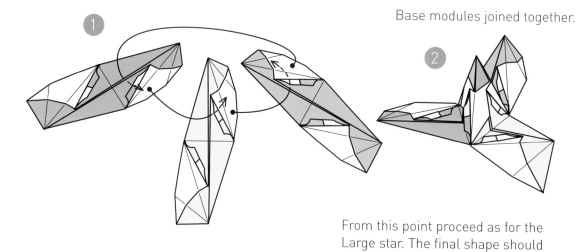

From this point proceed as for the Large star. The final shape should look like the adjacent photograph.

Paper:
standard
7.5 x 7.5 cm
(3 inches x 3 inches)

Morning glory

Relief shapes with a hole at the top will appear.
Using 30 modules will make a model that looks like a bunch of morning glories.

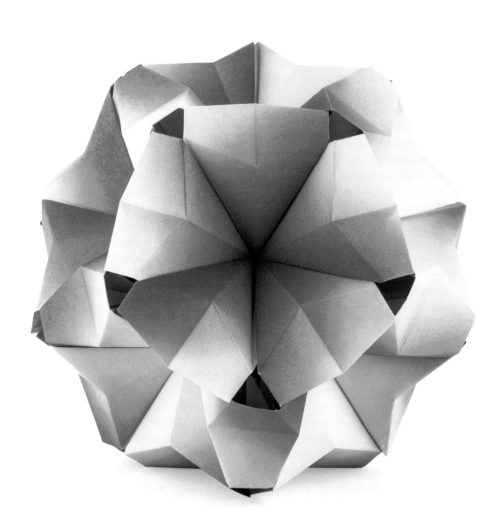

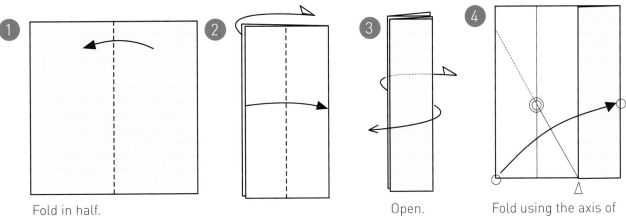

1 Fold in half.

2

3 Open.

4 Fold using the axis of the straight line marked by the △ symbol, bringing the O symbols together.

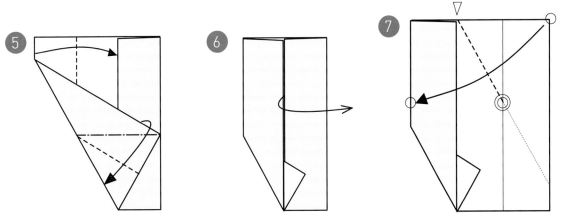

5

6 Fold using the axis of the straight line marked by the △ symbol, bringing the O symbols together.

7

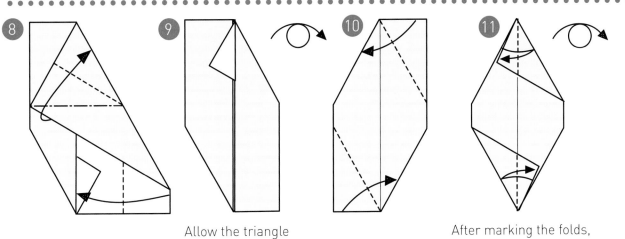

8

9 Allow the triangle to protrude.

10

11 After marking the folds, return to diagram 9 inserting the white triangle.

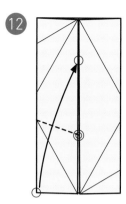

Fold to symbol ◎, bringing the 0 symbols together.

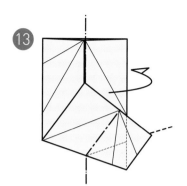

Fold the entire model in half and align with the line made by lifting in diagram 12.

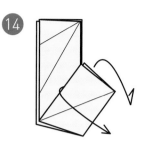

Take it back.

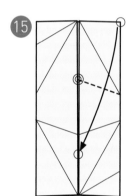

Also fold the other side as shown in diagrams 12 and 13.

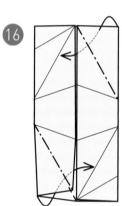

Inside reverse fold.

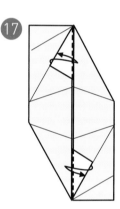

Keep the ★ symbol inside.

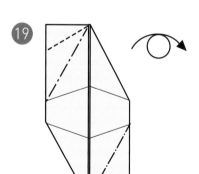

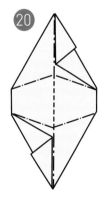

Shape by creating relief along the folding lines.

(x 30)

JOINING THE MODULES TOGETHER

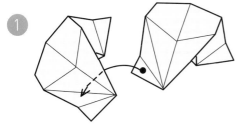

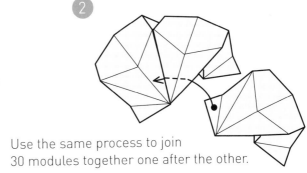

Use the same process to join
30 modules together one after the other.

Structure with 30 modules.

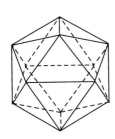

30 modules.

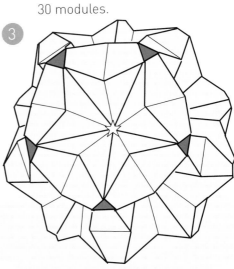

Join 5 modules together
in the hollow marked by
the ☆ symbol and 3 modules
at the points where the holes
are, to create triangles.

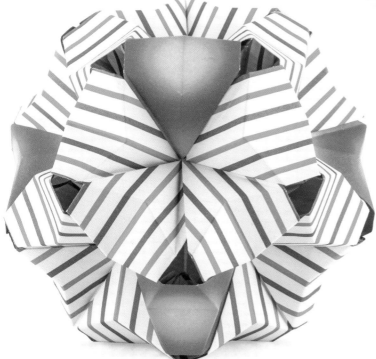